CLR STUDIES 10

Scaffold
Improving Training, Working Conditions, and Transformation in the European Scaffolding Sector

CLR STUDIES are publications of work
by the European Institute for Construction Labour Research
and its network of academics and practitioners,
and open to related contributions from all sources.

CLR
c/o EFBWW
Rue Royale 45
1000 Brussels
BELGIUM

© 2024 CLR
ISBN 978-0-9031097-4-1 (print)
ISBN 978-0-9031097-5-8 (e-version)

**Co-funded by
the European Union**

The content of this publication reflects only the authors' views, i.e. that of the partners in the SCAFFOLD project.
The European Commission is not responsible for any use that may be made of the information it contains.

Design: Beryl Natalie Janssen
Cover photo: VSB

Fernando Durán-Palma
Linda Clarke
Rolf Gehring
Jakub Kus
Christopher Winch
Maria Christina Georgiadou

Scaffold
Improving Training, Working Conditions,
and Transformation in the European
Scaffolding Sector

RESEARCH REPORT

TABLE OF CONTENTS

CONTRIBUTORS

PROJECT ADMINISTRATOR

Rolf Gehring — Political Secretary Wood and OSH,
European Federation of Building and Woodworkers (EFBWW)

RESEARCH COORDINATORS

Fernando Durán-Palma — Co-Director, ProBE, University of Westminster, UK

Maria Christina Georgiadou — Co-Director, ProBE, University of Westminster, UK

PROJECT EVALUATORS

Linda Clarke — Professor, ProBE, University of Westminster, UK

Christopher Winch — Professor, King's College London, UK

COUNTRY TEAMS

Belgium

Carine Callandt — Project Manager, Technical Competence Centre,
Constructiv, Brussels

Fabrice Meeuw — Director General, Building on People, *Constructiv*, Brussels

Willem Van Peer — Manager, Technical Competence Centre, *Constructiv*, Brussels

Denmark

André Breindahl — Collective Bargaining Officer, United Federation of
Danish Trade Unions *(3F Fagligt Fælles Forbund)*, Copenhagen

John Ekebjærg-Jakobsen — Chairman 3F Copenhagen, United Federation of
Danish Trade Unions *(3F Fagligt Fælles Forbund)*, Copenhagen

Thomas Strømsholt — Chairman, National Club of Scaffolders
(Stilladsarbejdernes Landsklub), Copenhagen

Esther Antreasyan Keller — Research Assistant, United Federation of Danish Trade Unions
(3F Fagligt Fælles Forbund), Copenhagen

Germany

Gerhard Syben — Research Institute for Employment Labor Qualification
*(BAQ – Forschungsinstitut für Beschäftigung Arbeit
Qualifikation)*, Bremen

Ireland

Brian McGann — IDEAS Institute, Dublin

Andrew McGuinness — Construction Sector Industrial Organiser, Services Industrial
Professional and Technical Union (SIPTU), Dublin

Mary Ogundipe — IDEAS Institute, Dublin

Netherlands

Hans Crombeen — Union Officer, Federation of Dutch Trade Unions
(*FNV Bouwen & Wonen*)

Gerard Westenbroek — Head of the Association, Dutch Scaffolding Association
(VSB - *Vereniging van Steiger-, Hoogwerk- en Betonbekistingbedrijven*)

Poland

Jakub Kus — Vice-President, Budowlani Trade Union
(*Związek Zawodowy Budowlani*), Warsaw, Poland

Tomasz Nagórka — Vice-President, Budowlani Trade Union
(*Związek Zawodowy Budowlani*), Warsaw, Poland

BOXES

Katrin Behnke — Project Officer, European Trade Union Confederation (ETUC),
Brussels, Belgium

Jean Marie Branstett — Former Chairman of the EFBWW OSH Coordination Group,
Force Ouvrière, France

Frank Krolle — Director of Studies, *Fritz-Henßler-Berufskolleg*,
Dortmund, Germany

Kristin Köhler — Subject teacher and Erasmus+ Project Manager,
Fritz-Henßler-Berufskolleg, Dortmund, Germany

Rob Miguel — National Health and Safety Advisor, UNITE the Union, UK

Christian Schlette — SDU Centre for Large Structure Production (LSP),
University of Southern Denmark, Odense, Denmark

Lex Taylor — Visitor Experience Officer, Canterbury Cathedral,
Canterbury, UK

Vicky Welch — Off-shore Advanced Scaffolder, Newcastle, UK

ACKNOWLEDGEMENT

We are indebted to the many others who participated
in this project from a range of organisations across Europe.

FOREWORD

SCAFFOLDING CONSTRUCTION has changed in many ways over the decades. Materials, techniques, work organisation and applications have evolved and become more complex. Working conditions, qualification requirements and training standards have also changed accordingly. To summarise, one could also say that the sector has become more differentiated.

However, it should also be noted that many aspects of scaffolding construction have changed little or not at all. The work is all too often still hard and takes its toll on health. Vocational training is completely underdeveloped in many countries. Working conditions are often poor and employment is unstable. Forms of worker representation, collective bargaining agreements and a stable social dialogue are often non- or barely existent.

Against this background and in cooperation with active scaffolders, the EFBWW has repeatedly organised scaffolding conferences since the 1990s, which have dealt with these issues and the question of how working and employment conditions, vocational training and the social recognition of scaffolding and scaffolders can be improved. In addition, the aim has always been to promote fair social dialogue in the scaffolding sector.

The EFBWW has now carried out a project in cooperation with some of its member associations, with paritarian organisations in the scaffolding sector and with employers' organisations, which once again looked at the state of affairs in scaffolding.

The research report presented here, which is based on six country reports, shows emphatically that we have good reason to look again at the issues referred to above.

A foreword should not attempt to and cannot summarise or judge a research report. However, we can say that scaffolding continues to vary remarkably from one country to another, in all the aspects analysed. Nevertheless, progress is possible, and there are many examples in the report. Progress is also necessary, whether it is a question of vocational training, occupational health and safety, employment conditions, work organisation or social dialogue.

Particular attention must be paid to the fair and social organisation of the internal market. Services, the free movement of goods and freedom of movement must not lead to existing protection standards and working conditions being undermined and eroded. The good training of employees in scaffolding construction also plays a major role here.

The project has proposed further steps towards better training. The specific policy proposals in this regard, which also cover the areas of occupational health and safety, general working conditions, technical development and social dialogue, are set out in the policy recommendations. They aim at company practitioners as well as the social partners and the political level.

However, there is still a long way to go to achieve the same high standard of working conditions and training levels. We suspect that the EFBWW has not carried out its last project for the sector.

We hope that readers will find this report interesting and that it will inspire them to further develop and improve work and working conditions in scaffolding sector.

Rolf Gehring / Tom Deleu

FAIR BUILDING, Polish Pavilion at the Biennale Architettura 2016, exhibition view.
Photo by Maciej Jelonek

The Polish Pavilion addressed the ethical issues facing one of the most underrepresented participants in architecture: the construction worker. Labour conditions, lack of respect and site accidents plague the industry worldwide but these difficulties often get overlooked.

1. INTRODUCTION

1.1 Aims of the SCAFFOLD project

The SCAFFOLD project, *Improving Training, Working Conditions and Transformation in the European Scaffolding Sector*, aims at the improvement of working conditions and the quality of vocational education and training (VET), as well as seeking progressive changes in work organisation related to the implementation of new technologies. Additionally, the project aims at improving the Social Dialogue within the sector as a precondition for a just evolution in terms of working conditions. Possible perspectives on gender equality are intended to be considered in general, especially in connection with technological innovation and possible changes in the work organisation of scaffolding work. Based on the insights provided, the project aims to prepare Policy Recommendations for the various fields that shall serve for improved discussions between the social partners of the sector. A final objective is to consider the feasibility of establishing a European Occupational Safety and Health (OSH) Certificate for Scaffolders. To achieve these objectives, the project includes the preparation and running of topical workshops, involving expertise from other stakeholders.

1.2 Previous initiatives

The SCAFFOLD project builds on a long tradition of international conferences organised by the European Federation of Building and Woodworkers (EFBWW) and held between 1996 and 2005. The first and second European Scaffolding Conferences were held in Denmark in 1996 and the Netherlands in 1997. The Third International Conference of Scaffolders (EFBWW, 1999) was held in a training centre in Weiterstadt near Darmstadt in Germany in October 1999, where at the time, over 20,000 persons attended courses each year. The conference was attended by 50 scaffolders from 10 European states – Austria, Belgium, Denmark, Finland, France, Germany, Netherlands,

Norway, Switzerland, and United Kingdom – and addressed the themes of bargaining and employment policies, OHS and VET.

The Fourth Conference of European Scaffolders (EFBWW, 2001), held in Belgium in 2001 at the time of the introduction of the Directive on Working at Heights, was attended by 60 scaffolders from 12 European states, including this time also participants from Italy, Spain and the Czech Republic. It concerned the needs:

o for a European standard for training, including OSH.

o to take account of economic and political conditions, including self-employment, fixed term contracts, illegal working, and the use of migrant labour.

o to consider the interlinkage of product development and standardisation requirements and for training to consider these together.

o to ensure proper implementation of the 2001 Directive at national level, including minimum requirements for a competent person.

o for a 'site-specific wage', also covering those from lower-wage areas of the European Union (EU).

o appropriate training, including OSH training and risks to the muscular-skeletal system with respect to the functioning of the spine due to back damage, as well as problems of exhaustion.

At the conference, it was reported that 10% of all occupational accidents are falls from height, with 10% of these causing permanent disability or death. Across the EU, these falls occurred to 500,000 people per annum and resulted in 1,000 fatalities, with the most serious accidents occurring in the construction industry.

A key means to reduce such accidents is through careful training and, on this issue, the 2001 conference flagged up three very different models of training for scaffolding:

1. *Denmark:* where in 1997 it was required that no one should erect or dismantle scaffolding over 3 metres without specialist training, leading to considerations for a 2-year scaffolding course. This course was revised in 2000, was for those over 20 years old only, and consisted of 16 alternating modules, 8 in a school setting and 8 practical, covering system and frame scaffolding, first aid, specialist scaffolding, the scaffolding business, scaffolding covers, and coordinated scaffolding erection, as well as a lorry course for scaffolding transportation.

2. *UK:* requiring a minimum of six months site experience for a Basic 'system' card, with a Scaffolder course of 2 weeks, and a further one week to become a 'Basic Scaffolder',

3. *Germany,* stretching over 3 years.

These three models are still evident today in the SCAFFOLD project.

Finally, the Fifth EEBWW Scaffolding Conference (EFBWW, 2005), held nearly 20 years ago in Eastbourne in UK in January 2005, was intended to assess the implementation, application, and operation of the 2001 Working at Heights Directive, with participation from Belgium, France, Germany, Netherlands, UK and Sweden, as well as the European

First European Scaffolding Conference, Copenhagen, 13–16 March, 1996
Courtesy of Thomas Strømsholt

Construction Industry Federation (FIEC) and manufacturers such as Layher, Peri and Hertel. This conference produced recommendations, including:

- requirements of a competent person for supervision, assembly, fixing scaffolding in place, users, including minimum knowledge to assess risks, safety measures needed, maximum loads permitted.
- for installation and assembly, erectors should be competent to assess suitability of ground, ensure parts arrive safely, determine dimensions and forms for type of work and weight involved so as to work safely and ensure components do not move.

In evaluating the situation for scaffolding twenty years later for the SCAFFOLD project, therefore, it is important to keep in mind the objectives and often lengthy and detailed discussions from these earlier conferences, to avoid repetition, and to assess how far the issues raised then and the recommendations drawn up have been addressed.

1.3 Context of the SCAFFOLD project

Much has happened in the subsequent twenty years, which suggests that changes that have occurred since in the labour market, in the construction industry, and specifically in the scaffolding sector, need where possible to be considered, including:
1. An ever-greater use of a migrant workforce and temporary work.
2. Increased fragmentation of the structure of employment through self-employment and subcontracting.
3. Digitalisation and even robotisation of many processes.
4. Added impetus for greater equality, diversity, and inclusion, particularly given the white-male dominated character of the construction industry.
5. The challenges of climate change and meeting zero carbon / energy targets set for the industry through zero carbon building and retrofitting.
6. Increasing challenges to initial VET (IVET) systems in providing good work-based experience, and greater demands for continuing VET (CVET) for the existing workforce.
7. An ever more complex and abstract construction labour process, placing added emphasis on quality assurance, inspection, monitoring, and enforcement of regulations.

The present research report provides information about the overall economic situation of the sector, the employment and working conditions with some focus on occupational hazards, the VET systems in the six participating countries – Belgium, Denmark, Germany, Ireland, the Netherlands, and Poland – and in Europe, and more specifically OSH training, changes in the technical composition of scaffolds and tools used and the related standardisation of work, also regarding digitisation and robotisation in scaffolding activities, and the social dialogue related to scaffolding.

1.4 Methodology

The main assumption of the SCAFFOLD project is that overall conditions in the scaffolding sector, and especially working conditions including OSH, are determined by framework conditions such as forms of employment as well as by more specific aspects such as the quality of VET, the overall technological development of the sector, the strength of Social Dialogue structures and differences in all these conditions between EU countries. The project, therefore, aims to analyse the current situation and identify potential areas for action within these across six European countries – Belgium, Denmark, Germany, Ireland, the Netherlands, and Poland.

The chosen methodological approach is both comparative and participative, involving systematic analysis of similarities and differences across countries and active collaboration with stakeholders throughout the process, covering the following key activities and deliverables:

1. Drafting of *national reports* by separate teams of researchers, to provide an overview of the situation in each participating country in terms of employment and working conditions, VET and OSH training, technological developments and Social Dialogue.
2. *Evaluation* of country reports by an external team of evaluators.
3. Dedicated one-day *workshops* for each of the four domains in which the country teams, experts and other stakeholders compare the situation of participating countries and discuss possible areas of action.
4. Special *visits* to the Dortmund-Mengede Scaffolding Training Centre in Germany and the University of South Denmark to gain better understanding of the central role played by VET and the potential implications of new technologies respectively.
5. Organisation of a *final conference* to discuss project findings and possible policy recommendations.
6. Production of the present *comparative research report* on the overall situation of the scaffolding sector across the participating countries based on information and insights provided by the national reports, the evaluation report, four workshops, two visits and final conference. The research report is put together participatively by an external coordinator.
7. Regular *reporting* in related structures of the EFBWW (Standing Committee Building/Coordination Group on OSH) and within the European Social Dialogue for the Construction Sector, including feedback rounds. This continuous process of internal evaluation is accompanied by the work of an external evaluator.
8. Formulation of *policy recommendations* for the various fields that shall serve for improved discussions between the social partners of the sector.

While the project's methodological approach offers numerous benefits, particularly in terms of enhancing understanding of similarities and differences in scaffolding across national contexts and encouraging critical reflection about ways of seeing and doing things, it also presents challenges. These include issues of conceptual equivalence (to what extent concepts being studied have the same meaning across different contexts), data availability (to what extent data on accidents, for instance, are available and comparable), language and translation (to what extent the meaning of words and phrases are equivalent), and interdisciplinary collaboration (bringing together experts from different fields and countries with different approaches, terminologies, and research traditions, which can be stimulating but also demanding).

Partly due to these challenges, the national reports underpinning this report exhibit considerable variation Some national teams relied exclusively on desk research, while others employed interviews and surveys to collect primary data. The national reports also vary in tone, with some more academic and others less so, and in extension, with some lengthy and others concise. This unevenness should not be viewed as a weakness;

rather, it reflects the diversity of approaches and insights each team contributes. Consequently, while the current research report offers a comprehensive introduction to the scaffolding service sector in Belgium, Denmark, Germany, Ireland, the Netherlands, and Poland, no claim is made that the information presented is exhaustive or definitive.

The present research report is organised into six sections:
1. *'What is scaffolding?'* provides background to scaffolding as an occupation, labour process, physical structure, and socio-economic sector, as well as key regulations affecting its functioning.
2. *'Employment and working conditions'* is about the sector's overall economic situation, employment, and working conditions with some focus on occupational hazards.
3. *'Vocational education and training and OSH training'* concerns the VET systems in the participating countries and, more specifically, OSH training.
4. *'Technological developments'* is about changes in the technical composition of scaffolds and tools used and the related standardisation of products.
5. *'Social dialogue in scaffolding'* refers to the social partner organisations, collective agreements, social dialogue arrangements, and paritarian organisations in each country.
6. presents the *'Policy recommendations',* stemming from the project.

SCAFFOLD Final Conference, Brussels, 4 June 2024
Courtesy of EFBWW

2. WHAT IS SCAFFOLDING?

This section provides necessary background to scaffolding as an occupation, labour process, physical structure, and socio-economic sector, as well as some key regulations affecting its functioning.

2.1 Scaffolding as an occupation

Scaffolding has been used since pre-historic times, including for Palaeolithic cave painting and the Egyptian pyramids, and then with bamboo for parts of the Great Wall of China. In the Middle Ages in Europe, it was needed for the building of cathedrals and abbeys, using wooden poles and hemp ropes. The word scaffolding stems from this period, from the French word *échafaudage,* referring to the raised wooden platform used for the public execution of criminals. Only in the early 1900s was the standard set of fixings for metal scaffolding introduced, patented in Britain by Daniel Palmer-Jones as 'rapid scaffixers' (1909) and then as 'improved universal coupler' (1918), with SGB (Scaffolding Great Britain, founded 1919) developing the first frame access system in 1944 and systems scaffolding used more and more from the 1950s and especially in the 1980s.

Throughout much of this period and throughout Europe scaffolding was generally carried out by, for instance, bricklayers or carpenters, in the course of the work being carried out on site, as it is still today in countries such as Poland. It was only after the second world war that it has become a specialist and recognised skilled occupation, for the purposes of training and OSH, going together with professional qualifications.

This process has been uneven involving, for example in the UK:

o   the Construction Industry Training Board (CITB), established in 1964, training scaffolders in its training centres.
o   the Construction Industry Scaffolders Record Scheme (CISRS), introduced late 1960s.
o   scaffolding being recognised in the National Working Rule Agreement as a skilled occupation from 1974, and
o   training developed in earnest from 1979 with formal Part 1, 2 and Advanced courses.

SCAFFOLDING YESTERDAY, TODAY AND TOMORROW: DENMARK

THOMAS STRØMSHOLT
Chairman, National Club of Scaffolders
(Stilladsarbejdernes Landsklub), Denmark

The scaffolding sector has often been viewed as conservative, marked by resistance to change and a strong adherence to the status quo. When I began nearly 25 years ago, the working day was markedly different. Site cabins were filled with smoke, and daily tasks were assigned with simple instructions. Education was reserved for the few, with learning primarily occurring through on-the-job training, where seasoned colleagues imparted their knowledge.

Today, the industry has transformed. Smoking is strictly prohibited, alcohol is absent from the working day, and education has become a central facet of professional life. Scaffolders report to modern facilities where tasks are meticulously planned and documented. Technology has made significant inroads with remote-controlled cranes, material hoists, and advanced safety equipment. All new employees undergo a two-year training programme, ensuring they are well-equipped to manage both the technical and safety aspects of their work.

Looking ahead, we anticipate even more technological advancements. Lighter yet stronger materials will make the work less physically demanding, paving the way for more women to join the industry. Laser scanning and photogrammetry will become standard in planning and documentation, reducing the amount of necessary equipment and further enhancing the working environment. Concurrently, new regulations and technologies will ensure that safety remains paramount. The scaffolding sector is in constant evolution, and it is our responsibility to ensure this progression continues for the benefit of both employees and society at large.

In contrast, in Germany, scaffolding only became a recognised training occupation or *Beruf* in 1991 and was considered as a full *Beruf* in 1998, though formal scaffolding training dates back to the early 1970s.

This very unevenness has an impact on how we evaluate the situation in different countries today, as each has recognised the status of scaffolding as an occupation and introduced regulation and VET schemes for scaffolding at different periods.

2.2 The scaffolding cycle: scaffolding as a labour process

As outlined above, scaffolding only emerged in Europe as a distinct occupation in recent decades. In the past, scaffolding was usually a component of the occupational profiles of other construction occupations and lacked a distinct identity. Consequently, it is still to be found as a component in, for example, the Polish bricklayer qualification. The evolutionary development of scaffolding as an occupation has meant that its structure has not necessarily been formally demarcated. However, analysis of the work of scaffolders carried out in the SCAFFOLD project suggests that it is an occupation based on a cycle of activity. Not all scaffolding workers will participate fully in all aspects of scaffolding cycle but within the hierarchy of qualified scaffolding work we can identify the following functions, which are followed in a broadly consecutive way:

1. Scoping of work to be undertaken
2. Designing and planning of work and commissioning of necessary equipment and workforce
3. Selecting, loading, transporting, and unloading scaffolding parts
4. Erection of scaffolding structures
5. Inspection, monitoring, maintenance, and modification of structures
6. Dismantling of structures
7. Removal and disposal of structures
8. Evaluation of work undertaken
9. Concurrent with the above and particularly in relation to 3 and 4 there will be an inspection, often carried out by a senior scaffolder with a specialist qualification.

A clear cycle of work is notable throughout the reports on the different countries involved, from scaffolding erection to alteration or modification, and then dismantling. What is unclear is whether training is specifically in place for the alteration part of the cycle and for the maintenance of the scaffolding. Denmark is exemplary in its implementation of the Working at Heights Directive and having high requirements for each phase of the cycle, though major accidents are generally attributed to poor planning.

Broadly speaking the 'scaffolding cycle' is a species of project management. Like other forms of project management, the cycle involves different knowledge (e.g. physics), know-how or 'skills', and competence (e.g. communication). The most obvious are these connected with the selection, erection, repair, maintenance, modification, dismantling and transport of the physical components of scaffolding, involving measuring, testing, fastening, hoisting, unloading etc. But, due to the complexity of the cycle, the following are also required:

- *Planning:* designing and working out the scaffolding structure and the materials and workforce needed to accomplish it.
- *Control and co-ordination:* ensuring that activities take place in sequence and that materials and workers are in place at the appropriate times.
- *Communication:* ensuring that information, questions, orders are delivered and understood in a timely and accurate manner (written as well as spoken).
- *Co-operation:* ensuring that workers interact productively with each other to achieve a common result.
- *Problem solving / identifying setbacks:* equipment failures and shortages, injury and sickness in the workforce, changes in client specification, vagaries of weather and ground conditions and working out solutions, including solutions that involve co-operation, communication, and co-ordination among members of the team.

Some countries, Netherlands and Belgium in particular, have substantial occupational hierarchies, with worker autonomy and supervisory responsibility increasing up the hierarchy, eventually including planning and co-ordinating large teams on complex sites. In these countries, competence at the lower levels of the hierarchy is more limited with more limited involvement in all aspects of the cycle. If this is an accurate representation of the core activities of scaffolders then health and safety, occupational subclassifications and IVET and CVET need to be derived from their role within the overall scaffolding cycle.

The most developed form of VET is the three-year German *Ausbildung in Gerüstbau* (VET in Scaffolding), described thus:

"Duration: 3 years – What does this occupation involve?
Scaffolders fit facades with working and protective scaffolding. They select the required scaffolding components, load them using lifting equipment, transport them to the construction site and assemble them. If necessary, they level the ground or attach load bearing supports before assembly. They assemble system components and anchor the scaffolding to the building. In special scaffolding construction, they not only erect the usual scaffolding on houses, but also erect special constructions such as supporting scaffolding as a substructure for concrete formwork, e.g. for bridge construction, or mobile working platforms, e.g. on high-rise buildings. When the scaffolding is no longer needed, they dismantle it professionally. They store the scaffolding parts and maintain them."
(Source: *Beruf Aktuell 2023-4, Bundesagentur für Arbeit*).

This description, intended for prospective scaffolders describes the scaffolding cycle but without specifying in detail the more advanced kinds of knowhow needed.

2.3 Scaffolding as a physical structure

Scaffolding as a physical structure, or 'scaffold', refers to a temporary and elevated work platform and its supporting structure used to support workers and materials during the construction, maintenance and / or repair of buildings and other human-made structures, providing access to heights and areas that would otherwise be hard to reach. Modified scaffolds are also used for formwork and shoring, grandstand seating, concert stages, viewing towers, exhibition stands, ski ramps and art projects. This section provides a general introduction to scaffolding materials, components, types, and technological development.[1]

There are three main types of *materials* used to make scaffolding. Wood was the most common scaffolding material used in Europe up until the 1920s, but has since been replaced by steel and aluminium and steel. The only scaffolding component still typically made of timber is the working platform or board. *Steel*, the most common material in the modern scaffolding sector, can support very heavy loads and is also flexible, though susceptive to corrosion and heavy to carry. Aluminium, in contrast, is much lighter than steel, making it easier to handle, and is resistant to corrosion, but has reduced weight stability due to its lightweight nature and is significantly more expensive.

Scaffolds are built using a variety of *components*, varying widely depending on the type of scaffolding used, specific job requirements, and broader environmental conditions. However, there are fundamental scaffolding components forming the basic structure of any scaffold, including:

1. *Base plates* (or sole plates) are the load-bearing base of a scaffold used to distribute weight and support the vertical scaffolding poles (standards). Connecting the base plates to standards ensures a strong scaffolding foundation. Base jacks, usually made out of steel and adjustable to various lengths, provide vertical height adjustment of the standards.
2. *Standards* (or uprights, verticals, legs), the long vertical tubes that transfer the load of the scaffold to the ground, are usually connected to base plates to ensure equal distribution of the load and are commonly made of either painted steel, galvanised steel or aluminium.
3. *Ledgers* (or runners) are steel or aluminium tubes running horizontally along the length of the scaffold, supporting the working platform, and determining the height at which the working planks (decks, boards) are staged. Ledgers are placed in between each standard and parallel to the building.
4. *Transoms* (or bearers, putlogs), horizontal components that meet the ledgers at right angles, provide support for standards and the working platform by holding them in position.

---

1 This section draws liberally from publicly available information from scaffolding service provides, producers and other businesses such as Avontus (2024).

5. *Boards* (or decks, battens, planks) form the working platform on a scaffold and are made of wood, aluminium, aluminium frame with plywood board, or galvanised steel.
6. *Fittings* (or couplers, clamps, clips) are the steel components connecting and holding the structural components of a scaffold together.
7. *Braces* are diagonal galvanised steel tubes reinforcing the scaffold's rigidity.

There are several *types* of scaffolding, distinguishable according to the material they are made of (wood, steel, aluminium, or bamboo), whether they use the building's structure as support or standalone (single or double frame scaffolding), or whether they are anchored in the ground, hang from an overhead structure or roll along (supported, suspended or rolling scaffolding), among many others. Common types of scaffolding referred to here include tube and fittings and system scaffolding.

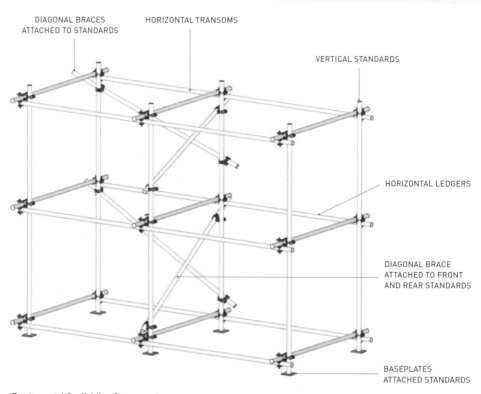

Fundamental Scaffolding Components
Abdel-Jaber *et al.* (2022)

Tube and fittings scaffolding (or traditional scaffolding, tubular scaffolding, tube and clamp scaffolding, or tube and coupler scaffolding) is assembled using individual tubes and various fittings. As its name indicates, fittings are extensively used in tube and fittings scaffolding. Tube and fittings remains the most widely used type of scaffolding in UK.

Systems scaffolding (or modular scaffolding) consists of posts with prefabricated fixed connection points, to which runners, bearers, and diagonals can be connected at predetermined levels. Systems scaffolding drastically reduces the need for fittings through

Tube and fittings (above left) vs Systems scaffolding (above right)

New technologies: Alimak's scaffolding transportation system
Courtesy of VSB

PEDESTAL AND SINGLE-ROW SCAFFOLDING: 15TH CENTURY

Scaffolding can be held up, without ground support, by bolts (beams) set into the wall. More often, however, the end of the bolts, opposite the wall, rests on a row of vertical poles (or stilts) set at regular intervals. Longitudinal timbers, run parallel to the construction, linking the poles in the same row and supporting the bolts.

This type of scaffolding, known as "foot scaffolding" (fixed to the wall) and "single-row scaffolding", is extremely stable and can even support lifting equipment.

Flavius Josèphe, *Les Ancientnetés des Juifs* (*The Ancients of the Jews*), circa 1480
© Bibliothèque nationale de France

SCAFFOLDING IN THE 17TH CENTURY

On this 17th-century building site, scaffolding is just as rudimentary and lacking in safety measures as on medieval sites.

Étienne Martellange (1569–1641), draughtsman
© Bibliothèque nationale de France

SCAFFOLDING IN THE 20TH CENTURY

On this reconstruction site for the *Printemps* department store in Paris, destroyed by fire in September 1921, scaffolding now combines wood and metal. Aerial cranes were used to lift materials.

Little by little, the industrialisation of the building industry also affected scaffolding techniques: scaffolding was made of metal (often steel), according to standard norms. The various scaffolding parts were gradually all reusable. In the early 1920s, English engineer Daniel Palmer-Jones patented the tubular metal scaffold: from then on, the parts fitted into each other, ensuring maximum stability.

However, it was not until the 1950s that safety standards became more widespread: construction sites were gradually equipped with guardrails, shoulder harnesses, reserved perimeters...

© Bibliothèque nationale de France

these built-in connections and predominates in the participating countries. There are several types of system scaffolding including *Cuplock, Kwikstage,* and *Ringlock,* and proprietary types like *HAKI, PERI UP, BrandSafway, Layher, AT-PAC, Scafom-Rux* and *Turner OCTO.*

The history of scaffolding is a narrative of continuous *technological development* driven by the need to enhance efficiency, ensure worker safety, and adapt to changing demands. Until well into the Industrial Revolution, scaffolding in Europe relied on wooden poles and ropes. The introduction of iron and steel in the 18th and 19th centuries increased the strength and durability of scaffolding structures, and the production of standardised components at the turn on the 20th century improved safety and efficiency, while allowing for taller and more complex structures. The introduction of modular scaffolding systems like Cuplock and Kwikstage in the 1950s and 1960s represented another leap forward, offering superior improvements in assembly speed, safety, and flexibility.

Today, scaffolding technology continues to evolve in all areas. Interesting developments include, but are not limited to, the adoption of *labour relieving tools and machinery* to reduce the physical strain on workers such as electric lifts, hoists, cranes, and trolleys; *advanced individual and collective safety features* such as fall protection systems and advanced guardrails; *integration of lightweight materials* like aluminium; *digital planning tools* like Avontus Designer and Viewer; and *sensor systems* optical scanner systems that monitor stress, weight load, and environmental conditions in real-time to maintain structural integrity, issuing warnings if necessary.

The field of robotics and artificial intelligence offers a window into the future. Innovations potentially revolutionising the sector include: *drones* with sensors for monitoring scaffolding safety or construction progress; *exoskeletons* to support and enhance human movement by providing mechanical assistance to the body; *cobots,* or collaborative robots, designed for safe collaboration with humans while maintaining high productivity such as KEWAZO and Infineon's *Liftbot*; and scaffolding *robots* designed to automate the assembly, inspection, maintenance, and disassembly of scaffolding structures. However, the potential impact of technological developments lies, by definition, in the future, and so, while it is not possible to determine with any certainty whether a particular innovation will be broadly adopted and / or stand the test of time, these and other developments are a testament to the ingenuity and dynamism of the scaffolding sector.

SCAFFOLDING YESTERDAY, TODAY AND TOMORROW: FRANCE

JEAN MARIE BRANSTETT
Former Chairman of the EFBWW OSH Coordination Group,
Force Ouvrière, France

Ever since humans first began constructing buildings, scaffolding has been one of the essential elements for working at heights. Starting with wooden and bamboo scaffolding, which is still used today, manufacturing techniques have evolved considerably.

Yesterday:

Scaffolders used tubular steel scaffolding, the weight and complexity of assembly of which made the work very arduous. You had to do the bracing yourself, the floors were made of wood and difficult to handle, and you had to assemble it all while always being at risk of accidents. Then there was the difficulty of getting the equipment to the right level, usually by hand, which made the job even harder.

Bulk loading into lorries required a lot of unnecessary handling, with risks of entrapment or bumping during loading or unloading.

Learning was done on the job, and safety rules were not always respected. PPE was fairly basic and sometimes uncomfortable or even dangerous, such as belts instead of harnesses.

Today:

Scaffolding has evolved towards aluminium, bracing is integrated into the frames, there are handling aids of all kinds, and MDS scaffolding allows scaffolders to be safe for most of their working day. Preparing the site with installation plans, stability calculations, etc. .... helped the scaffolders and saved them time in both the preparation and assembly phases.

Transporting the equipment in specially adapted containers has eliminated the need for a lot of handling and ensured that the equipment remains stable during transport.

Compulsory training incorporating safety rules, and PPE adapted to the tasks to be carried out and adapted to the human being, have considerably added to the attractiveness of a profession that nevertheless remains very physically demanding. →

Future:

Where everything has yet to be invented.

We must continue to lighten the equipment without reducing its strength, use 3D simulation to install the equipment in an optimised way, innovate in the accessories needed to ensure difficult passages, integrate lifts on scaffolding of more than 5 levels (we can dream!). Try new lightweight materials (composite), always with the aim of taking the drudgery out of this profession.

Monitor and check scaffolding with drones, especially after major weather events.

Continue to train people to make them more autonomous and to learn to economise intelligently.

Open up the profession to women, even if this can only be done if the weight of equipment changes significantly.

2.4 Scaffolding as a socio-economic sector

A 'sector' refers to a distinct part of the economy characterised by a specific kind of economic activity. Sectors are typically categorised into three main types: primary (extraction and harvesting of natural resources), secondary (manufacturing and industrial processes that transform raw materials into finished goods), and tertiary (provision of services rather than goods). While scaffolding is closely related to, and typically associated with, industries such as construction, oil and gas' downstream activities, energy, shipbuilding and civil engineering (which are secondary sector activities), the actual provision, setup, and maintenance of scaffolding is a service, making it part of the tertiary sector. Partly as a result, defining the exact boundaries of the 'scaffolding sector' is challenging.

One possible way of doing this is by identifying the sector's main actors, that is, the range of entities that contribute to the provision of scaffolding services. These include, most obviously, scaffolders and scaffolding companies, but go beyond to involve construction companies, both as direct employers and contractors and subcontractors, the Social Partners – workers' representative organisations (unions) and employers' associations – paritarian organisations, regulatory and safety bodies, and clients and end-users that, in addition, to secondary sector industries also include primary and tertiary activities, such as oil and gas' upstream activities, and entertainment and event-related structures. Relevant actors also include scaffolding manufacturers and producers of scaffolding related products such as software, lifts, and climbing gear.

2.5 The regulatory framework

The current regulatory framework in Europe that either encompasses scaffolding or could potentially, is important to understanding the nature of scaffolding and to drawing up recommendations related to the work and training of scaffolders.

2.5.1. Regulating working at height

Of relevance to the SCAFFOLD project is the fact that scaffolders are expected to be able to demonstrate that they can meet at least the minimum requirements of the Working at Heights Directive (Directive 2009/104/EC of 16 September 2009), originally Directive 2001 (45/EC). This Directive concerns 'the minimum safety and health requirements for the use of work equipment by workers at work' and is 'a single Directive within the scope of the OSH Framework Directive'.[2] Meeting these minimum requirements usually involves certification as proof of competence gained via both IVET and CVET routes. The Directive covers all occupations involved in working at heights, including but not confined to scaffolding, and continues to provide the main legislative framework for the scaffolding sector across Europe. It applies even in UK, where it has been maintained since Brexit largely because, as elsewhere, falls from height remain the largest cause of fatal accidents, representing in the UK 13 of the 30 fatalities in construction in 2021/2, though only one of these was attributable to scaffolding. In UK too, in 2022 manual handling was the most common cause of injury in construction, then slips and trips, whilst out of a scaffolding workforce of 17,315, there were 67 accidents reported.

2.5.2 Regulating occupations

The EU has a variety of instruments for the regulation of occupations some of which are mandatory regulations predominantly applied to occupations with safety critical aspects. Scaffolding is certainly such an occupation. However, it is not a regulated occupation in the way that, for instance, nursing or heavy goods vehicle driving are, so it is important for the SCAFFOLD project to consider whether scaffolding could not come under similar regulation. With nursing, for example, European Directive 2005/36/EC for Health and Social Care Professions regulates the number of hours to be devoted to theory and practice, as well as the broad content of the curriculum in terms of scientific knowledge, clinical experience and ethical conduct (Brockmann et al., 2011). This type of regulation is 'input oriented', primarily concerned with the content of the curriculum

2 https://osha.europa.eu/en/legislation/directives/3
   Consulted 13.11.23

and that the qualification reflects mastery of that content. Another partly input-oriented example is the Certificate of Professional Competence (CPC) required for heavy goods vehicle drivers under European Directive 2003/59/EC 'Initial Qualification and Periodic Training for Drivers of Road Vehicles for the Carriage of Goods or Passengers', which like the nursing qualification specifies length of training and includes theoretical and practical elements. Like the nursing regulations, the CPC is in effect also a licence to practise.

Unlike regulated occupations such as nursing, however, for which necessary inputs in curricula and qualifications are specified to ensure professional competence, other European tools can be described as 'output-oriented', such as ESCO (European Skills, Competences, Qualifications and Occupations), intended to promote European labour market mobility by providing a standard classificatory approach to skills, competences, and occupations. ESCO has constructed a vast number of occupational profiles based on aggregating task-based skills and competences from the Skills Pillar to form occupations.[3] There are two scaffolding occupational profiles offered by ESCO: the *Construction Scaffolder,* who "puts up scaffolds and platforms in order to make safe construction work at heights possible" and is identified with 17 essential skills and one item of essential knowledge; and the *Construction Scaffolding Supervisor* who "plans and supervise the transport, assembly, disassembly, and maintenance of the structures [and] ensures the safety of the scaffolds, support structures, access ladders and fenders" and is identified with 24 essential skills and the same item of essential knowledge, 'scaffolding components', as the construction scaffolder.[4]

However, ESCO does not provide a solution to the problem of constructing a common standard for the European scaffolder. The descriptions fail to refer to the scaffolding cycle outlined and the holistic and integrated nature of scaffolding work involving project management, teamwork and problem solving. The ESCO construction scaffolder has little autonomy and, while some of the essential 'skills' referred to are highly specific such as 'recognise signs of wood rot', others are highly general, such as 'follow health and safety procedures in construction'. The ESCO occupational profiles thus tend to adopt a 'lowest common denominator' approach, often falling below national standards, but also veering between highly specific and highly general skill descriptions (Mottweiler *et al.*, 2020).[5] Furthermore, they are based on an aggregative model of assembling occupations by adding skills, thus exposing the profile to the risk that the component parts add up to less than what is required by the whole (Winch, 2021).[6]

---

3   https://esco.ec.europa.eu/en/classification/skill_main

4   https://esco.ec.europa.eu/en/classification/occupation_main

5   https://lit.bibb.de/vufind/Record/DS-185603/Preview

6   https://apprenticeships.blog.gov.uk/2017/08/01/apprenticeship-frameworks-and-standards-the-main-
    differences/

One further element of EU law concerning mobility of employment adds weight to the urgency of developing a common standard that does justice to the work of the scaffolder. EURES, the European Employment Portal. (REGULATION (EU) 2016/589)[7] is expected to be incorporated into national law and sets up an updateable database whereby, through the instrument of ESCO[8], employers can specify job requirements and prospective employees can determine whether their competences and qualifications match these. Compared to the occupational profiles of scaffolders in the countries in this study, however, which contain often very detailed and substantive content and are more than descriptions of required actions, the ESCO profiles are too narrow, not mentioning scaffolders working independently or solving problems and largely limited to behavioural specifications.[9]

In summary, in relation to European regulation:
- Scaffolding is not a regulated occupation but subject to EU regulations concerning important aspects of the work of scaffolders, above all working at height.
- Only minimum standards of equipment and action are covered.
- Scaffolding is given a non-mandatory ESCO-based description based on specified skills in the EURES platform.

2.5.3. Regulating health and safety

The EU does not enjoy competence in VET and thus in harmonising vocational qualifications, though it can make recommendations and construct instruments in which members participate voluntarily. However, there are areas relevant to scaffolding where EU law does apply, including OSH, where, since scaffolding is a safety critical occupation, the 'reach' is considerable:
- The *European Framework Directive on Safety and Health at Work* (Directive 89/391 EEC) adopted in 1989 guarantees minimum safety and health requirements throughout Europe while Member States are allowed to maintain or establish more stringent measures.[10]
- 2001/45 – *Amendment of Council Directive 89/655/EEC* concerning the minimum safety and health requirements for the use of work equipment by workers at work (second individual Directive within the meaning of Article 16(1) of Directive 89/391/EEC).[11]

7 https://eur-lex.europa.eu/legal-content/EN/TXT/?uri=uriserv%3AOJ.L_.2016.107.01.0001.01.ENG
   Consulted 13.11.23

8 https://eur-lex.europa.eu/legal-content/EN/TXT/?uri=uriserv%3AOJ.L_.2016.107.01.0001.01.ENG
   Consulted 13.11.23.

9 https://esco.ec.europa.eu/en/classification/occupation_main#overlayspin
   Consulted 15.11.23. Note that the Scaffolder is a five digit occupation within the ESCO classification.

10 https://osha.europa.eu/en/legislation/directives/the-osh-framework-directive/the-osh-framework-directive-
   introduction
   Consulted 13.11.23

11 https://www.eumonitor.eu/9353000/1/j9vvik7m1c3gyxp/vitgbgi928gz
   Consulted 13.11.23.

Though not necessarily rigorously enforced, there are thus legally binding minimum standards for the putting up, maintenance and use of scaffolding structures.

As well as implementing EU directives, states can supplement EU directives legislatively if desired, as well as issuing non-binding guidelines. Crucially national agencies are also ultimately responsible for enforcement of regulations, although the EU conducts periodic audits of national practices, including oversight of CVET relating to OSH as well as inspection and enforcement of regulations in the workplace. For these there need to be occupational inspectorates well enough staffed and funded to carry out their role. OSH also applies to scaffold users as well as scaffolders, though national accident statistics for scaffolding do not necessarily distinguish between scaffolding workers and other workers.

CHANGING
THE PUBLIC'S PERCEPTIONS
OF SCAFFOLDING

LEX TAYLOR
Visitor Experience Officer, Canterbury
Cathedral, England

I love Scaffolding. Scaffolding is often seen as an eyesore, a nuisance, a sign of decay.
But what if we could change our perceptions and appreciate scaffolding as a symbol of care,
preservation, and renewal? Especially when it is protecting heritage buildings like Canterbury
Cathedral, one of the oldest and most beautiful cathedrals in England.

Scaffolding is not only a temporary structure that supports workers and materials during
construction or repair. It is also a way of showing respect and love for the history, culture, and
architecture of our ancestors. It is a way of ensuring that these buildings can survive the test
of time and continue to inspire generations to come.

It is not ugly; it is beautiful. It is a sign of progress, of innovation, of creativity. It is a way of
adapting to the changing needs and challenges of our society. It is a way of honouring the
past while embracing the future.

Next time you see scaffolding around a heritage building, don't frown or complain.
Smile and admire. Scaffolding is not a problem. It is a solution.

Scaffolding on
Canterbury Cathedral,
England, dating back
to 11th century

Photo: Marci-stock.adobe.com

3. EMPLOYMENT AND WORKING CONDITIONS

3.1 Overview

3.1.1. Employment conditions

Scaffolding is a small sector of the construction industry, estimated to employ between 0.5 to 1.5 % of construction workers across the countries studied[12], though this does not distinguish scaffolders, off-site workers, or employed and self-employed. The size of most companies in the sector is also small, even micro, with fewer than 49 employees. Terms and conditions of employment and how they are determined vary, ranging from countries with comprehensive sectoral collective agreements and high coverage, such as Denmark, to countries with narrow firm-level collective agreements and low coverage, such as Poland, to countries where common terms are established by law, such as Ireland.

Whilst employing a growing number of migrants, the scaffolding sector is in other respects not diverse, particularly in terms of gender, having everywhere very low levels of participation of women, significantly lower than the already low proportion of women employed 'on-site' in the construction industry. It tends, too, to be an ageing sector and one regarded as unattractive in terms of working conditions.

3.1.2. Working conditions

The numerous safety and health risks posed to workers mean that scaffolding remains one of the most dangerous parts of the construction industry across the countries studied. Due to the lack of reliable and comparable data, however, it is impossible to precisely establish the frequency, severity and development of accidents affecting

12 Estimate calculated using data from country reports over total employment in construction in Belgium (210,000), Denmark (184,350), Germany (2,650,000), Ireland (167,300), Netherlands (487,000), and Poland (500,000). Sources: FIEC, Danmarks Statistik; Destatis; CSO; and Euroconstruct respectively

SCAFFOLD WORKSHOP 1: WORKING CONDITIONS IN THE EUROPEAN SCAFFOLDING SECTOR

Brussels, 22 November 2023

LINDA CLARKE
ProBE, University of Westminster

This current project was initiated by the Dutch colleagues because of free movement and the lack of training, the minimum level of OSH training possible and qualifications, though some standards are in place. A contrast was drawn between the Finnish situation, dominated by small firms, with many migrant workers, and where there is little training, and the Danish, where everyone must go through the 2-year training programme, including migrants.

The nature of competence needed was discussed, the standards necessary, and the possibility of a European certificate for scaffolding. In terms of definitions of competent persons, there are different perspectives, that of the scaffold fitter, the user, and the supervisor. A competent person also needs to approve the scaffold. A former German labour inspector spoke of the importance of having competence to carry out the work. Risk assessment must be prepared by the contractor and subcontractors for the client, and it is important to make sure the supervisor is up to it; this is the responsibility of the employer. It is also necessary to supervise the use of the scaffolding. The user must not alter the scaffolding as any modification needs a competent person. In Poland, though the person inspecting is connected with the scaffolding company, in practice there is no clear responsibility and norms and standards are partly European safety measures, with OSH standards set by law but with shortcomings. What is the regulation for scaffold inspection regulation – is supervision with the scaffolding company or the contractor? It was concluded that minimum standards and a definition of scaffolding are needed.

Further areas where policies are needed concern statistical data, awareness, and entry into the sector, as well as occupational diseases associated with scaffolding. Other issues discussed included OSH certification, different qualification levels, scaffolding in other areas such as offshore and in shipyards, and recognition of scaffolding, especially in Poland where there is also no collective agreement.

scaffolders, though lack of supervision and lack of the qualifications required are given as important reasons for accidents. A key issue is that available statistics do not differentiate between scaffolders and users of scaffolding, often overestimating the number of accidents affecting scaffolders themselves. The sector also poses numerous health risks to workers, not least because of considerable physical demands placed upon them, including general physical overload, heavy lifting, and weather exposure. As a result, scaffolders generally cannot reach retirement in good health, so making scaffolding employment sustainable for workers should be a priority. Despite the considerable health risks that scaffolding poses to workers, there are no officially recognised occupational diseases for scaffolders across the countries studied; nor are there available data on scaffolders' level of absence related to occupational diseases. However, data from Denmark indicate that most diseases affecting scaffolders are musculoskeletal.

3.2 Employment and working conditions in scaffolding in different countries

3.2.1. Belgium

Employment conditions

In Belgium, in 2022, 41 scaffolding companies employed 1,724 employees (1,463 blue-collar and 261 white-collar), representing 0.78 % of workers employed in the Belgian construction industry. Most companies in the scaffolding sector (88 %) are small or micro, employing fewer than 49 employees. Employers interviewed indicate a growing demand for scaffolding services, though total employment in the sector has remained largely stable in recent years. Between 2018 and 2022, the number of scaffolding employers rose from 35 to 42, whilst the number of 'blue-collar' workers decreased from 1,598 to 1,463 and 'white-collar' workers increased from 214 to 261. The number of scaffolders seeking employment in 2021/2 was relatively high, though employers reported difficulties finding suitable candidates. However, word of mouth is the dominant recruitment channel in the construction sector and few job vacancies were detected in 2021 and 2022 by the public employment service, which itself only reflects about a quarter of construction companies' labour requirements.

Employers interviewed indicate that they mainly work with their own personnel on standard contracts, numbering 1,310 blue-collar and 261 white-collar in 2022, supplemented by temporary workers, numbering 80 and 164 respectively, and a small number of posted workers. While 1 % of all construction workers are female, the ratio of female scaffolders is only 0.3 %, ranging between 3-6 individuals between 2018 and 2022.

The construction industry social partners set minimum industry rates according to:

a. *wage category of workers,* whereby the gross hourly wage for qualified and experienced scaffolders (3 years) belonging to wage category III on 1 July 2023 was € 19.452.

b. *risk of occupational accident,* whereby the social partners have established a system of wage supplements based on the risk incurred, for instance when scaffolding is erected and removed at heights of more than 10 meters scaffolders receive a 10% pay supplement and at a height of more than 15 meters 25%.

Working conditions

According to data from *Constructiv,* there are no significant differences in the frequency of accidents between the scaffolding sector and the overall construction industry in Belgium. However, absence resulting from accidents is generally above the average for the whole industry indicating that, when they happen, accidents are more serious. There are no data available on scaffolders' level of absence related to recognised occupational diseases, and there appear to be no increased risks in the scaffolding sector for most of the diseases on the list, such as caused by chemical agents, infectious diseases, etc., though a few diseases caused by physical agents, whilst not recognised, might be considered.

Hazards reported and measures taken to address these include:

- *exposure to UV radiation* when routinely working in sunlight, for which workers should stay hydrated throughout the day and take frequent breaks in a cool area, preferably indoors, and work should be scheduled during cooler hours when possible.

- *exposure to weather conditions* (low or high air temperature, rain, snow, wind), for which measures including shovelling snow, waiting for temperatures to rise, and use of tarpaulins should be considered.

- *disorder and untidiness and falling objects,* for which workers should be trained to recognise the hazards of a cluttered work area and encouraged to maintain a tidy workspace.

- *traffic and passers-by,* for which adequate barriers should be provided to prevent impact from vehicles and sufficient measures taken to prevent unwanted interactions with passers-by, and noise.

- *working at height,* for which workers should wear PPE including safety harnesses, especially when working at heights greater than two meters, except when collective protection is present and with appropriate authorisation. The safety harness should be securely anchored to a suitable point, and workers should be trained to use the harness properly. Other protective equipment (helmet, work clothes) must be worn that is suited to the work.

Drawing up and maintaining a Safety and Health Plan is always mandatory for temporary or mobile construction sites for which a 'coordinator-design' or a 'coordinator-realisation' must be appointed and where one or more high-risk works are carried out.

To improve working conditions, there is a focus on migrating to lighter materials, training in the working position for lifting heavy materials, and adopting lifting tools. The adoption of lifting tools includes the use of cranes, telehandlers, material elevators, exoskeletons, and liftbots to hoist heavy materials during the erection and disassembly of scaffolds. *Constructiv* has also produced *information and sensibilisation tools* for scaffolding companies to improve prevention when assembling and using scaffolding. Some examples are:

o   Prevention sheet U009 Use of façade scaffolding in the workplace,
o   Toolbox sheet 2055 Use of façade scaffolding on site,
o   A code of good practice for the assembly and use of scaffolding,
    drawn up on the initiative of social partners and the government.

More consideration is also given to ergonomics, both in the office and on site.

3.2.2 Denmark

Employment conditions

In Denmark, there are approximately 1,500 trained scaffolders. However, the figures for those in employment vary depending on seasonality, mobility between industries, source and methodology. In 2022, the Danish Construction Industry Association included about 70 scaffolding member companies, employing around 1,300 scaffolders, though this number rises to about 2,000 in the summer months. The industry generally has a low unemployment rate, but employment is seasonal; in March 2023 the union records 119 unemployed scaffolding workers, down from a peak of more than 400 in 2020, with employment standing at just under 1,400 workers, up from about 1,250 in 2020. There are only a small number of self-employed individuals and temporary agencies using migrant labour, lower than in the rest of the construction industry owing to the high degree of organisation and unionisation (94%) in what is a relatively small sector with a strong community that can identify companies that exploit the use of migrant labour. 2% of those employed in construction are women, but the 'number of female scaffolders can be counted on one hand', and an incentive is being created to encourage more women to enter the industry.

Scaffolders' employment conditions are regulated primarily by the Building and Construction Collective Agreement between the employers' association of scaffolding companies and the 3F trade union, stipulating a 37-hour working week, with most scaffolders working on a piecework basis, that is pay by performance, known as the *Akkord* system. The collective agreement is a so-called minimum wage agreement, whereby wages are negotiated locally at least once a year, though, in practice, it is often the case that wages are negotiated at the start of each new construction site. The typical gross hourly wage agreed for a scaffolder in the Capital Region of Denmark, excluding the employee's and employer's pension contribution, Collective Agreement social supplement, benefits and irregular payments, piecework-related payment, and bonus payments, was in the last quarter of 2022 DKK 252 (c € 40), whereas for the Construction industry it was DKK 216 (c € 30) in the same quarter. The high volume of performance-based pay and the organisation of the scaffolding sector are seen to drive up wages and to contribute to more thorough planning of the work.

Agreements are reached between the parties on pricing for the *Akkord* system and the collective agreement provides rules for its performance. The price list covering the entire scaffolding area is a collection of prices and payments for work performed, down to a unit price for each part, and includes industry-specific rules and agreements. Any new scaffolding parts or changes in methods are discussed and negotiated in an ongoing process, a so-called price list committee with representatives from both the Scaffolding Section and the scaffolding workers' national association. OHS initiatives are a natural part of this work and are included in the pricing process. For instance, to promote a better working environment and reduce wear and tear, prices and payments have been reorganised to make the use of heavier scaffolding equipment more expensive, so creating a motive to invest in lighter equipment and utilise lighter parts.

Working conditions

The scaffolding sector has one of the highest accident rates in Denmark. The average accident incidence rate in 2022 was 240 per 10,000 FTEs (full-time equivalent employees), for building and construction just under 600, and around 1,300 for the scaffolding sector. However, as the incidence rate covers all accidents related to work on scaffolding and not just accidents to scaffolding workers, the statistics very likely over-represent. The Scaffolding Association conducted an in-depth analysis of 112 accidents in the industry from 2003-2008 showing that most accidents (48%) had occurred on the ground, with vehicles and in contexts where they could be attributed to poor planning; only 5% were directly related to frame fencing and scaffolding assembly; 38% were in and on the scaffolding and so had nothing to do with frame fences or falls; and 8% occurred on rolling scaffolding, which is not erected or used by scaffolders but by other construction professionals.

The National Club of Scaffolders *(Stilladsarbejdernes Landsklub)*, Denmark, constantly emphasises the importance of reporting all accidents to obtain accurate statistics, a policy slow to develop in other parts of construction and other industries so that the number of unreported accidents may be higher elsewhere. There are no recognised occupational diseases for scaffolders, but the Danish Working Environment Authority has a subgroup, 'other manual labour', that includes scaffolding workers, where most diseases are musculoskeletal. Associated occupational diseases reported (i.e. not necessarily recognised) are musculoskeletal disorders (55%), skin diseases (14%), ear diseases (11%), mental illness (8%), respiratory diseases (3%), cancer (1%) and neurological diseases (5%). There are, however, no data available on scaffolders' level of absence related to recognised occupational diseases.

To address the OSH risks posed to scaffolders, employees must be protected from external influences, such as weather conditions. Employers are required to provide PPE for the given weather conditions according to OSH legislation and to protect employees from exposure to, for example, solar radiation. Scaffolding work in cities and traffic areas creates major nuisances and challenges when it comes to the working environment and safety of scaffolders, including in establishing welfare facilities such as toilets, sheds, etc. and storage space for equipment or securing scaffolding contractors by cordoning off work areas. Traffic flow considerations are prioritised, often resulting in scaffolding being erected from the back of trucks or with only a limited working area, causing inconvenience to scaffolders. In cities and urban areas, scaffolding contractors also must beware of road users such as cyclists and pedestrians, requiring special attention to their safety when erecting scaffolding. There are also traffic flow considerations on motorways under the Danish Roads Directorate so that to work on these roads completing a course on the Road as a Workplace is often required.

The social partners in the scaffolding sector have a key role in preventing accidents and attrition and have long focused on physical wear and tear and ergonomics and how the physical working environment can be improved. The trade union 3F, the employer organisation *Dansk Industri Byggeri* and the Danish Working Environment Authority have approved and implemented three action plans, acting as a lever to constantly improve the working environment by focusing on: minimising loads using technical aids for manual vertical transport, horizontal transport and loading and unloading of vehicles; full fall protection; and using lighter scaffolding equipment.

o *Action Plan 1 (2005)*, intended to minimise loads caused by manual handling, where technically and economically feasible both horizontally and vertically, using technical aids for manual vertical transport, horizontal transport, and loading and unloading of vehicles.

o *Action Plan 2 (2011)* concerns the implementation of the EU directive on work at height, requiring full safety for scaffolders during assembly and dismantling of scaffolding. The plan has an adaptation track relating to full fall protection in all open fields, including making it mandatory for scaffolders to wear harnesses when assembling and dismantling column and frame scaffolding, as well as additional measures. The development track is aimed at strengthening OSH efforts in the scaffolder training programme.

o *Action Plan 3 (2019)* focuses on reducing the overall physical strain when erecting and dismantling scaffolding, including fully implementing Action Plan 1 and involving employees in OSH planning in the company and changing pricing in the *Akkord* system. The plan, implemented in the 2023 Collective Bargaining agreement negotiations, makes it more expensive to erect heavy scaffolding equipment, so giving employers a financial incentive to use lighter scaffolding to prevent attrition in the sector. A survey conducted in 2019 to identify scaffolding workers in the sector to strengthen retention showed that: the average age is around 38 years and the average scaffolder has been in the sector for around 11 years; there are geographical differences in education level and use of technical aids, in particular that, on average, cranes or similar technical aids were made available on 64 % of the cases with scaffolding work, ranging from 91 % in North Jutland to 38 % in South Jutland.

It is a statutory requirement to elect a work environment representative in companies with ten or more employees, and on construction sites with five employees from the same company for a duration of more than 14 days. These are tasked with participating in preventive OSH work in the company, including making use of technical aids based on the action plans, etc.

The parties also jointly finance the *Industry Community for the Working Environment* in Construction focused on improving the working environment throughout the construction industry, including running the *Construction Industry Working Environment Bus,* which visits construction sites and shares best practices for an improved working environment, and holding an annual Working Environment Meeting around the country. The Danish Working Environment Association for the Construction Industry has also produced industry *guides* for scaffolding, reviewed and approved by the Danish Working Environment Authority, setting OSH guidelines meeting legal requirements, covering:

o   Erecting and dismantling scaffolding.
o   Standard blades for system scaffolding.
o   Construction site roads – scaffolding access roads.
o   Industry guide on fall protection equipment.
o   Set-up, dismantling and use of trestle scaffolding.
o   Set-up, dismantling and use of wide rolling scaffolding.
o   Use of work platforms.

For these, the social partners provide joint guidance on current OSH issues, so that they express the social partners' common understanding of what constitutes good standards and practices within the sector.

VISIT TO SCAFFOLDING COMPANY IN DENMARK

Visit arranged by the union 3F and
hosted by Michael Kirk, *Herlev Stillads*,
June 2023

LINDA CLARKE
ProBE, University of Westminster

All new employees are enrolled in the 2-year formal scaffolding training, beginning with a 3-week course and then undertaking a series of eight modules, varying in length from 5 to 15 days, plus 5 weeks truck and lorry training, totalling in all 110 days. First the employee/ apprentice learns about construction and regulations, how much a deck can hold etc., and then they practice it; after 2 years they can read from the manual. The company employs someone for 3 months and then there is an exam; after the first course, workers mainly work at the lower level. There are three in a team. Out of 1,467 scaffolders trained, there have been about 3 women. The state pays for some trainees, though less per hour. The training each worker has undergone is carefully mapped. Some courses are international, in English, and English is becoming the main language in the firm too, though some go to Danish school in the evenings.

Scaffolders work under the *Akkord* system. Workers earn a basic, say £6 per hour, which can be 15-30% of total earnings, so that then for a skilled worker the *Akkord* can be 70% of earnings. Half the workforce is paid per hour. Workers work a 37-hour week, beginning at 6.15am and working for 7.4 hours per day. Dismantling is 50% of the *Akkord*, and loading and unloading is also part of *Akkord*. After the first 3 months, workers go on *Akkord*, receiving 40% if new and if experienced then 60%. There are not enough experienced scaffolders and

Scaffolding with hoist on Copenhagen refurbishment site

Well-protected scaffolding platform
on Copenhagen refurbishment site

more supervision is needed. Workers are of different nationalities, including Palestinian, Polish, Venezuelan, Lithuanian, Nigerian, and Somalian. At one time they had 30 new people, half were trainees and half experienced. People also come to the firm having worked in scaffolding for a few years but without training. Everyone is in the union, including migrant workers. There are hardly any accidents from falling, especially because for high scaffolding there must be a fence. Most accidents are in the yard with the forklifts.

The firm does not use any traditional scaffolding. The scaffold is no longer so heavy; with the old system you could not change the width or depth, and it was heavier, in a fixed rectangle, so increasingly inflexible. Bricklayers, for instance, need a wider scaffold. The gap between the wall and the scaffold cannot be more than 30 cms. Poles can be long, 1.5 metres or 1.25, and planks are 10 cms wide; there are lighter planks and heavier poles. Scaffolding is more and more complicated especially as, for instance, windows can be very heavy. Scaffolding used is steel, though aluminium is lighter, and the firm does have some wooden planks. There have been lots of changes over the past 15 years. Hoists, for instance, first introduced in 2003, are much safer, there are small cranes, and forklift trucks are quicker. Trucks are all diesel, not yet illegal. The firm's yard is very well equipped, including rectangular frames, poles, planks, couplers and clamps, whilst inside there is a range of PPE.

The company mostly services renovation projects, not so much new build, and at the time of the visit had 23 projects. For each project they work out the type of scaffolding needed, including the weight for the type of building, the trucks needed and hoist, what power and canteen are in place, plus manual transport and calculation of the *Akkord* payment system. Everyone then gets instructions. A large site visited, for instance, employed 4-5 scaffolders, was originally built in the 1950s and is undergoing renovation/retrofit. A security and work environment coordinator looks at different projects and each site is checked 2 or 3 times, and marked, either yellow in progress or green as checked. A 'work environment report' is then produced.

Complex scaffolding on roof
of Copenhagen refurbishment site

Photos: Courtesy of Linda Clarke

3.2.3. Germany

Employment conditions

In Germany, the 2022 annual basic statistical survey of the construction industry counted around 2,600 scaffolding companies, employing about 35,000 and generating a total turnover of € 3.5 billion. Micro scaffolding firms, with less than ten employees, represented 60 % of the sector. Construction activity, as everywhere in Europe, is anticipated to weaken due, for instance, to inflation and the increased cost of credit, despite a great demand for housing, with the *Hauptverband der Deutschen Bauindustrie* (German Construction Industry Federation) forecasting a 6 % decline in turnover in 2024. The situation in relation to the scaffolding sector is unknown, though this has remained largely stable in recent years, with a total number of employees of around 34,000 in 2023, registered unemployed 1,600, and registered vacancies around 800. In addition, under the Posted Workers Act, around 5,400 employees are working in scaffolding. The approximately 170 posting companies from the EU are mostly service providers working in Germany through contracts for work and labour or with employee-leasing permits; there is thus no employment structure as such for migrant labour in the scaffolding sector. In addition, the proportion of women in the sector is less than 1 %, mainly female entrepreneurs.

Working conditions

Scaffolding is still one of the sectors of the construction industry associated with high accident rates and an occupation that is not without danger to health. In terms of occupational diseases, these are not recognised for individual activities such as scaffolding, but for the entire construction industry, including noise-induced hearing loss and, since 2021, hip joint arthrosis and red skin cancer due to the consequences of strong sun exposure. In terms of occupational accidents, data collected and published by the employers' liability insurance association for the construction industry, *Berufsgenossenschaft der Bauwirtschaft (BG Bau),* record 88 per thousand full-time workers in 2021, lower than in 2018, at 100, and much lower than in 2012, at around 120. Though their frequency in scaffolding has decreased in recent years, it is still partly higher than the figures for other construction occupations. However, available figures do not allow sufficient conclusions to be drawn as to whether the accidents are in connection with the erection, conversion or dismantling of scaffolding (accidents involving scaffolders) or occurred during use (accidents involving scaffolding users). If work is carried out according to regulations, a scaffold erected by the scaffolder is taken over by an appropriately trained person – foreperson or site manager – when it is handed over to the scaffold user.

Data on lost work due to accidents at work are not available for individual occupations, such as scaffolding, but only for the overall construction industry, employing around 2.2 million people, where in 2021 an average of around 20 days of work lost was registered per employee due to accidents at work and, in total, 43.4 million working days could not be worked. The most frequent occupational accidents involving scaffolding are falls, not only falls from scaffolds but also from ladders and stairs or ceilings, as well as roofs with insufficient load-bearing capacity. The 2021 annual report of *BG Bau* highlights a significant decrease in fatal fall accidents compared to 2020, from 40 to 19. Accidents due to falls are frequently followed by accidents caused by falling or collapsing objects such as components, materials and loads, as well as accidents resulting from loss of control over supported, moved and handled components and materials. Other causes of accidents are slippery or obstructed floors. Finally, work on a scaffold's topmost level is risky and one of the most frequent sources of accidents if protective devices have not yet been fully set up. Progress on this was, however, achieved in 2018 with the new version of the Technical Rules and Regulations (TRBS), focusing on anticipatory side protection on the topmost scaffold level.

The hierarchy of OSH measures is referred to as the TOP principle (technology – organisation – person), which involves consistently implementing obligations described in the European Occupational Health and Safety Directive 89/391/EEC, requiring employers, for example, to avoid risks for their employees, assess unavoidable risks and combat hazards at source. Scaffolding has developed into an industry in which OSH in accordance with the TOP principle is high priority, requiring that technical protective measures (T) are always taken wherever possible when erecting, converting and dismantling scaffolding, and organisational measures (O) are taken if these are not possible. PPE (P) must be used if neither technical nor organisational protective measures are possible or justifiable. The TOP principle is consensus among the players in the scaffolding industry, helped by the efforts of the collective agreement parties in creating financial incentives to demand and encourage safety-conscious behaviour and its promotion for employees on construction sites and managers in offices. Scaffolders are generally unable to carry out their profession for longer than the age of 60. Consequently, the ergonomic quality of the scaffolds, especially the weight or its reduction, serves as a target variable in scaffolding design, development and manufacture. Vital rules provide guidance to workers and companies on safe behaviour and everyone in construction has the right and duty to say STOP! when a rule is broken.

Safety precautions generally slow down work initially, making it more expensive, while the economic benefits of safety only materialise in the longer term. If contracts are awarded primarily based on price, tenders in which realistic costs for effective OSH are calculated would have little chance without this consensus. The Contracting Rules for Award of Public Works Contracts (VOB/A) stipulate that the cheapest bid is not to be considered the most economical but rather economic efficiency results from an overall assessment including qualitative, environmental and social aspects.

3.2.4. Ireland

Employment conditions

In Ireland, no sector-specific data on the number of scaffolders employed are available. Nevertheless, there is a legal requirement for construction workers to attend a safety awareness training programme managed by the national training authority, SOLAS, and to renew this certification every four years; during the four years 2019-2023, 4,162 workers attending this programme identified as scaffolders. There are also no official available data on the types of contracts that scaffolders are employed under though the union experience is that specialist scaffolding contracting companies employ many scaffolders directly on full-time permanent employment contracts, whilst a small number are employed by main contractors and through employment agencies. However, how smaller scaffolding sub-contracting companies and companies posting their employees in Ireland employ scaffolders is unknown. Anecdotal evidence suggests that what is known as 'bogus' self-employment, applying to those classified as 'self-employed' but to all intents and purposes 'employed', is rampant and growing as a share of employment in the construction industry. The proportion of female scaffolders is unknown, but figures for the construction industry show that, while 46 % of 'off-site' construction workers are female, only 1 % of 'on-site' workers are.

Employment conditions in the construction industry are regulated through the Sectoral Employment Order (SEO) (Construction Sector) 2021, which came into effect on 1 February 2022 and places a legally binding floor on rates and obligations and defining what activities place an employer within construction and what experience and qualifications place a worker in a particular employee class. The law on SEOs is set out in the Industrial Relations (Amendment) Act of 2015, which provides the legislative basis. The SEO has a dispute resolution procedure, requiring that employees first raise individual disputes with their employer at local level, the employer being obliged to respond within five working days. If not resolved, the dispute can be referred to the Workplace Relations Commission, whose decisions can be appealed to the Labour Court. Under the current SEO, scaffolders who hold an Advanced Scaffolding Card and have four years' experience are classified under Category A Workers and entitled to a rate of € 21.59 per hour from August 2024, while category B workers receive € 20.03.

Working conditions

No specific figures regarding accidents in scaffolding are available, but data for the construction industry show that work at height remains the greatest factor for fatalities and serious injury in the construction industry; of the 10 fatalities recorded in 2021, 7 were falls from height. Specific causes of scaffolding-related accidents include:
o   Substandard boards (HSA, 2014)
o   Scaffold boards that were not secured adequately and inspected
o   Overturning of access tower or contact with electricity lines

o Falling from height
o Dropping of tools or scaffolding components
o Lack of PPE
o Construction and dismantling of scaffolding by incompetent / untrained worker
o Tripping over objects and wet surfaces
o Collapsing of scaffolding resulting from rusting parts and construction
   by an inexperienced person (HSA, 2018).

No data are available on the level of absence of scaffolders, though for the overall construction industry the Labour Force Survey records work-related injuries and illnesses causing four or more days of absence from work. Whilst fluctuating considerably from year to year, this indicates that construction's rate of injuries fell from 24.4 per 1,000 workers in 2006 to 15.5 per 1,000 workers in 2020 (HSA, 2022).

The Safety, Health and Welfare at Work Act 2005 and the associated Schedule 3: General Principle of Prevention require employers to manage and conduct work activities in such a way as to ensure the safety and health of their employees; to provide systems of work that are planned, performed and revised as appropriate to be without risk to health; and to implement measures for the protection of the safety and health of their employees. To assist compliance, the Health and Safety Authority (HSA) provides useful resources and guidance to promote better working, for example, on Managing Ergonomic Risk in the Workplace to improve Musculoskeletal Health (HSA 2019), highlighting the risk and actions to be taken by employers and employees. For instance:

o Regulation 97 of the Guide to the Safety, Health and Welfare at Work (General
   Application) Regulations 2007 also requires that 'an employer shall ensure that
   work at height is carried out only when *weather conditions* do not place the safety
   and health of employees at risk'. Scaffolders are at risk of falling from height if
   there are ice and snow on the platform, for example, for which full check of all
   platforms and fall / edge protection, de-icing of work platforms, wearing proper
   clothes, drinking plenty of fluid, and increased calorie intake are recommended
   (HSA, 2010).
o In areas above *pedestrian traffic*, particularly above entrances into the structures
   and building or above where people are working, preventive measures include
   using brick guards to prevent outward movement, sheeting to prevent materials
   from passing through, and safety fans to retain and prevent objects that may
   accidentally fall from the structure, protecting pedestrian traffic areas and access
   points (HSA, 2018).
o The scaffold should also be protected from *vehicular traffic* by appropriate warning
   signs, lights, barriers, or traffic cones. Where vehicles are permitted to park
   adjacent to the scaffold, the risk of damage to the scaffold is high, vehicle damage
   should be avoided by preventing such parking or providing barriers, and, where
   this is not practicable, the scaffold should be inspected frequently so that damage
   may be detected and remedied.

SCAFFOLDING YESTERDAY, TODAY AND TOMORROW: IRELAND

ANDREW MCGUINNESS
Construction Sector Industrial Organiser,
SIPTU, Ireland

Scaffolding in the Ireland of the past was seen as a labourer's job, and anyone could do it. But as buildings got higher and scaffolding jobs more difficult, the old wooden pole and lashings began to be replaced with tube and fittings and prefabricated scaffolding systems. When I returned to Ireland in the early 1990s prefabricated systems were mainly used, also the number of components for the systems were limited and heavy. Fall protection for scaffolders was never a consideration when planning or doing a job. But with an increasing number of pharmaceutical and technology companies setting up in Ireland, and several protests by workers to make construction sites safer places to work, a cultural shift in the thinking around health and safety started to emerge. Mandatory training and assessment for scaffolders was introduced, a code of practice for scaffolding was developed, and prefabricated scaffolding systems that have an endless number of components started to be used.

Scaffolders in Ireland today are trained and certified to a national standard. Fall protection is a must. Jobs are planned, and drawings for complex scaffolds to be erected are becoming more commonly used by scaffolders. However, the scaffolding sector still faces its challenges today; the physical demands scaffolding imposes on a person's body and whether scaffolding provides secure and rewarding employment that constitutes an attractive and worthy occupation are two of the challenges. The development and rollout of the scaffolding apprenticeship in 2021 with level 5 certification on the National Framework of Qualifications is seeking to address in part some of these challenges, but the sector still lacks direct engagement with scaffolders, particularly in the area of design and manufacturing of scaffolding systems.

The future of scaffolding in Ireland looks positive, provided the sector embraces technological advances that enhance scaffolding as a career choice, continues constantly reviewing the standards of training, health and safety, and engages in social dialogue at National, European, and international level. The introduction of the scaffolding apprenticeship in Ireland will also provide new opportunities for career progression and pathways to lifelong learning.

o   *Interaction among occupations / different work activities* taking place on scaffolds requires proper scheduling of activities to ensure that the scaffold is available and safe to use when needed and that the activities of an individual trade do not endanger the scaffold or other users of the scaffold (HSA, 2018).

The *Code of Practice for access and working scaffolds* provides practical guidance to scaffold erectors, contractors, and users of scaffolding on the requirements and prohibitions set out in the relevant statutory provisions. The high rates of activity and change on construction sites, together with high level of risk associated with scaffolding work, are seen to require a correspondingly high level of safety management to prevent accidents and ill health. Thus, the Code of Practice provides a practical template for the systematic management of scaffolding operations (HSA, 2018), giving recommendations and guidance on the erection, use, inspection and dismantling of simple access and working scaffolds, as well as on the training and instruction of those erecting, dismantling and using scaffolds. The National Access and Scaffolding Association (NASC) provides further guidance including:
o   SG4:15 Preventing Falls in the Scaffolding Industry.
o   TG20:13 Guide to Good Practice for Tube and Fittings Scaffolding.
o   TG4:11 Anchorage Systems for Scaffolding.
A further improvement is that equipment must follow product standards.

3.2.5. The Netherlands

Employment conditions

In the Netherlands from 2015, employment in the construction industry increased by 80,000 full-time jobs, more than 20,000 of these between 2021 and 2022, completely reversing the substantial employment losses during the banking and euro crisis. In the report *Trends op de bouwarbeidsmarkt 2022 – 2026*, the Economic Institute for the Construction Industry (EIB) also describes how shortages in the construction labour market have increased markedly since the start of the coronavirus crisis, with 81 vacancies per 1,000 employees recorded in the second quarter of 2022, a third more than the peak in 2019 and double the 2020 level. The performance of the scaffolding sector is closely linked to that of the construction industry, although some activity is linked to the industrial production sector.

   In 2023 the Dutch Association for scaffolding companies consisted of about 60 scaffolding member companies active in construction and in the petrochemical, steel, food, offshore and energy industries. Many more small scaffolding or construction companies employ their own scaffolders, whilst many self-employed either take on work themselves or are hired by other (scaffolding) construction companies. In 2022, figures for the construction industry, which do not include scaffolders employed in industry or by temporary agencies, reveal 1,250 scaffolder employees and 1,510 self-employed scaffolders, with approximately 45.3 % employed on standard contracts, and 54.7 % self-employed (EIB, 2020-22). Migrant scaffolders in temporary jobs dominate in the Netherlands. Reliable figures for temporary and self-employed workers in scaffolding are, however, lacking, and unions and employers are in discussion about setting up a system that registers all workers on any given construction site, partly due to the shifting workforce, with many scaffolders coming from abroad and only in the Netherlands a short time. There is also a trend towards more flexible working in scaffolding, there being few permanent employees as companies hire temporary and self-employed workers and migrant scaffolders in temporary employment dominate. Few women, if any, are reportedly working in scaffolding.

Working conditions

There are no specific figures regarding accidents in scaffolding, only accidents concerning falling from heights, though these data include the users of more products for working on height, such as ladders and steps etc., and falling from (building) constructions. For scaffolders and scaffolding users, the main safety risks identified are falling from the scaffold when climbing, descending or working on it, being hit by equipment or materials falling from the scaffold, becoming trapped / crushed by equipment or materials during loading, unloading and assembly, and being unable to leave the work area because the escape routes are non-existent or inadequate. There are also risks for people walking or working near scaffolding, such as being hit by objects or materials falling from the scaffold and being injured by the scaffold collapsing or falling over. The four factors having major consequences for the safety of a scaffold are:
1. poor preparation in terms of calculations, drawing, reliability, and durability,
2. incorrect choice of scaffolding components, using materials from different scaffold types,
3. incorrect, incomplete or careless assembly of the scaffold,
4. incorrect use of the scaffold, for example by overloading or altering it without approval.

There are no recognised occupational diseases for scaffolders and their degree of absenteeism is not recorded separately. However, the scaffolding companies affiliated with the *Vereniging van Steigerbouw Bedrijven* (Association of Scaffolding Businesses, VSB) highlight sustainable employability problems that mean many employees cannot expect to reach the state pension age in good health (VSB, 2022). In addition to safety risks and the danger of falling, scaffolders face potential health risks as lifting heavy objects and lifting too often are especially bad for the body. The Scaffolding Guideline *(Richtlijn Steigers)* drawn up by the construction social partners contains recommendations for assembling, altering and dismantling steel static scaffolds, and especially for bringing in and removing materials, in a safe and healthy manner and for using them as a safe place for working at height. The back, shoulders and arms are particularly subject to heavy strain as workers usually perform their work standing, walking, bending over and / or kneeling. The main recognised hazards relate to weather and traffic, and the Guideline sets out how to act in these circumstances. Any persons working in scaffolding – whether in industry or in construction sector, be they employees, migrant or self-employed, etc – must be certified according to Scaffolding Guideline standards. Employers may deviate in principle but must prove that they have achieved the same or better / higher level of OSH than the Guideline, which is in practice impossible.

Many companies are opting to use lighter materials (aluminium instead of steel) and increasingly using labour-relieving tools such as forklifts, pallet trucks, cranes and mobile trailers / carts to move larger quantities of scaffolding material to, from and on the construction site. Small goods lifts are also increasingly being used to raise scaffolding material during assembly.

3.2.6. Poland

Employment and working conditions for persons employed in the construction industry are defined in the Labour Code. Conditions for scaffolders and scaffold users as well as supervisors are also set out in implementing OSH acts (regulations).

Employment conditions

In Poland, the economic performance of the scaffolding sector is closely linked to that of the construction industry, although some activity also relates to industrial production. Despite the pandemic, when the construction industry was not subject to lockdown, no significant reduction in economic activity was evident between 2019 and 2022; an increase in activity for small businesses could even be observed in 2020-2021 due to renovations and refurbishments. Interviews with scaffolding manufacturers indicate too that the pandemic period did not affect the scale of production of new scaffolding or the level of employment in manufacturers' companies. Nevertheless, in 2022, numbers employed in construction decreased from 1,030,636 in 2021 to about 948,000 by December due to the deteriorating economy.

There are no specific data on scaffolding companies or employees, though most companies are small, and their numbers do not exceed 600, based on internet portals offering scaffolding assembly services. Similarly, the number of workers employed in the sector can be roughly estimated, based on those with valid registrations as scaffolding operators and erectors, which as of August 2023 stood at 64,663 registered scaffolders (Warsaw Institute of Technology Łukasiewicz Network). However, registration is for an indefinite period and the register has not been updated since the 1970s, though it contains between 3,000 and 4,000 new entries every year from those who pass the theoretical and practical parts of the exam. There is no recorded employment of women in the sector.

It is difficult to estimate the different types of contracts under which scaffolders work not least because scaffold assembly is carried out by employees with other qualifications, for example bricklayers or roofers who also have a scaffolding assembly qualification. As an occupation scaffolding very rarely exists in isolation from other qualifications in the construction industry, though the scaffolding assembly qualification is usually additional to the employee's main qualification. Companies specialising in scaffolding installation very often also provide comprehensive renovation and refurbishment services. An important distinction can, however, be made between large companies providing services in the public sector, which are required by statute (2019 Public Procurement Law) to employ workers on standard contracts, and small businesses servicing the private sector, which tend to employ workers under civil law contracts, essentially a form of subcontracting. The Public Procurement Law also specifies requirements for the working conditions of persons performing construction work under public contracts involving scaffolding.

An important issue in the Polish construction industry is the (under)-employment of migrant workers from third countries. These are not included in statistics but, according to various sources, number between 160,000 and 180,000, 93 % of whom are from Ukraine. Most took up work in the industry based on the so-called employer declaration of the need to employ a foreigner (a procedure facilitating the employment of workers from several third countries of Eastern Europe) and are employed under contracts other than employment contracts. Without regulations recognising their qualifications, there are also no data on these.

Working conditions

In Poland, data from the National Labour Inspectorate's comprehensive study of accidents in the scaffolding sector show that in 2022, there were 122 accidents involving scaffolding, including a high proportion (16) of fatalities and serious injuries (27). The reasons of these accidents were:

- *technical* (19.5 %), predominantly due to lack of or inadequate collective protection measures (39.3 %) and / or inadequate safety devices (20.6 %).
- *organisational* (47.3 %), mainly attributable to lack of supervision (21.9 %) followed by tolerance by supervisors of deviations from OSH rules and regulations (11.2 %).
- *due to human error* (33.2 %), predominantly incorrect behaviour of a worker, including insufficient concentration on the activity being performed combined with the occurrence of an unexpected event (21.2 %), ignorance / disregard of OSH regulations and rules, and disregard of danger (bravado, risk-taking), followed by alcohol consumption and failure to use PPE.

The National Central Institute for Labour Protection produces recommendations, and the National Labour Inspectorate conducts campaigns and publishes instructions for trainers on the ergonomics of working with scaffolding. Conditions for working with scaffolding are set out in the Building Act, in OSH requirements and in other regulations for construction projects, defining, for instance, temperatures and exposure to weather, and forbidding erection of scaffolding during high winds and rain and in the vicinity of other structures being erected at the same time. Interviews indicate that companies are putting in place increasingly restrictive measures to monitor such circumstances on an ongoing basis. However, the decision to work on scaffolding under certain conditions always falls under the site manager's responsibility.

There are no recognised occupational diseases directly related to work on the assembly or use of scaffolding and scaffolding is not included in the list of work under special conditions or of a special nature. Occupational disease cases of an employee working with scaffolding can only be established through individual diagnoses not directly related to the nature of the work. Musculoskeletal loads, work at height and in harsh weather conditions do not formally have a direct bearing on assessing a worker's health or finding an occupational disease; nor are data available on occupational diseases. OSH in the construction industry is of particular interest to the Labour Inspectorate, the Labour Protection Council at the Polish Parliament, and the Ministry of Development and Technology, responsible for the construction division. Work is currently underway at this Ministry to update regulations on the safety of work on scaffolding – including those machines and equipment whose operation requires acquiring qualifications and descriptions and definitions of different types of scaffolding. The Labour Inspectorate prioritises working at heights in construction (including scaffolding), resulting in more inspections and prevention campaigns (Construction Stop Accidents Campaign, Build Safely competition for companies) with the participation of social partners.

Improvements, especially applying to large construction projects, include progressive elimination of old scaffolding systems, increased labour inspections, increasing use of drones in supervising scaffolding assembly and disassembly, and use of safety and PPE by workers. There is, however, little use of digital technologies in the design process of scaffolding assembly.

3.3. Comparing employment and working conditions

Though there are significant differences, it is apparent from the country reports that, in many respects, scaffolding has become more precarious and subject to flexible working through, for instance, self-employment, posted employment, temporary working contracts and the use of migrant labour than was evident in 2005. The Netherlands, for instance, reports a trend to 'flexible working' in scaffolding, with only 45% directly employed and 55% self-employed, more vacancies than job seekers, the employment of migrant workers in temporary jobs, and stagnant productivity growth. Denmark is notable for its high levels of unionisation (over 70%) in construction and regulation through collective agreement, though also reporting the use of temporary agencies and self-employment and a significant migrant workforce, many of whom have poorer

GENDER EQUALITY IN SCAFFOLDING

VICKY WELCH
Offshore Scaffolder Advanced, England

In a nutshell, the reason why there aren't many women scaffolders is the physical aspect. Scaffolding is a physically hard job. Although there are a lot more women out there now that can do the physical aspect of it (I've proved that because I'm not someone who goes to the gym and lifts high heavy weights, and I've managed) but there are things I've struggled with. This is the question nobody's ever asked. No management has ever said: Is there anything you struggle with? I've been treated equally, so I can't argue that I have been treated unequally. But we have differences with men. We're of equal value, but we aren't physically the same. This is not about bringing differences up. If you do, where does it end? But it's just about being realistic. Realistically, there are physical aspects of the job that I know we differ in. I have seen a change in scaffolding companies using lighter steel and aluminium, banning 21-foot tubes, and using system scaffolding, making the sector less challenging for women and more inclusive. Regulators must consider this if they also wish to see a more diverse industry.

You're not going to get women into scaffolding unless you are massively advertising and promoting women in the industry, college, any kind of education system, and also home, the way you are brought up – you're conditioned a certain way, and we are still in a generation where we are conditioned that scaffolding is a man's job. It's very hard for a woman to set foot, take courage, and step into an industry where you know you are going to be the minority. It's still a very intimidating industry to a woman. We still aren't seeing enough women. It's not really portrayed, though we're seeing it in media a little bit more. You're seeing it on posters now, when a lot of the companies, whenever they get a woman in, they'll use that as part of their media and their sales. But in reality, there's still a need; there's yet to be a movement to actually get to the people on the tools.

conditions, may be paid a minimum wage, and lack knowledge of the 'Danish model', especially of the *Akkord* wage system. In contrast, despite greater labour mobility in construction more generally, including many workers who use scaffolding, Belgium reports lesser mobility and low levels of self-employment and use of temporary workers in scaffolding. In Poland, the collective agreements do not specifically cover scaffolding and migrant workers can be authorised to instal scaffolding after passing an exam and having their qualifications confirmed, though their under-employment is extensive.

Scaffolding is usually carried out outdoors, exposing workers to the elements. Across the countries studied, similar environmental hazards (weather conditions, pedestrian and vehicular traffic, interaction with other trades or work activities, etc.) are recognised, but different combinations of prevention measures are reported, ranging from appropriate use of PPE (personal protective equipment) and collective protection to regular health examinations and specific training for particularly hazardous work and requirements, such as Denmark's 'Road as a Workplace' course. In improving the working environment, ergonomics also has an important role to play. Numerous OSH prevention initiatives by unions and authorities are reported, varying significantly, including the production of information and sensibilisation tools for scaffolding companies by the paritarian organisation *Constructiv* in Belgium, the joint development of action plans by the social partners in Denmark, financial incentives for safety-conscious behaviour and its promotion for workers and managers in Germany, the tripartite Code of Practice for access and working scaffolds in Ireland, and the Scaffolding Guideline in the Netherlands.

Considerable effort is also being made in some countries, including Belgium, the Netherlands and Germany, to use lighter materials and introduce new technologies to improve working conditions. In Belgium, there are wage supplements based on the risk incurred, for instance in working at heights above 10 or 15 metres, exposure to weather and noise and the use of harnesses. And in Denmark, the collectively agreed *Akkord* wage system is calculated to reward safe working. Due to the sector's working conditions, each country reports different control measures, including priority being given to working at heights in construction by the National Labour Inspectorate in Poland and the Contracting Rules for the Award of Public Works Contracts in Germany.

4. VOCATIONAL EDUCATION AND TRAINING AND OSH TRAINING

Vocational Education and Training (VET) for scaffolding figures prominently in the national reports and in all the workshop discussions held during the project, raising important issues for consideration in the recommendations.

4.1 What is meant by a 'competent person' in scaffolding

In all the national reports there is information concerning what constitutes a competent person in the scaffolding occupation. By 'competent person' we understand an individual capable of working to an expected standard in realistic conditions. Some countries, such as Germany, offer a generic competence concept that is more ambitious:

> "The overarching goal of vocational training is the ability to act in the workplace. This is understood to mean the ability to achieve the specified work result in the work process independently based on one's own understanding of the work objective and the given circumstances of the work performance without detailed instructions." (Syben 2023: 3).

Competence is generally assessed through the possession of certification and/or demonstration of onsite ability. There are different formal routes to competence ranging from a full initial VET (IVET) qualification for scaffolders, as found in Germany and Denmark, to continuing VET (CVET) based certifications, usually requiring more than one day of preparation for assessment, such as found in Belgium. In addition, some countries, for example Poland, include elements of scaffolding within other occupational profiles, such as bricklaying.

There is differentiation within scaffolding according to its complexity. To take the German example, a construction scaffolder achieves competence normally within three years of pursuing a Dual System qualification, divided between classroom, workshop or training centre, and work experience. A competent individual can erect (and presumably dismantle) all types of scaffolding using the appropriate materials and engaging in necessary preliminary work. However, more advanced scaffolding work involves broader competences, including planning and organising scaffolding construction, and supervising teams. Some countries such as Belgium also have distinct routes for scaffolding inspection.

Whether one or more occupations are involved, scaffolding requires competences that are hierarchically organised, ranging from construction under supervision (assistant scaffolder) to independent construction within a supervised team, to supervision of increasing large and complex teams onsite. Scaffolders work in teams, for instance of two or three as in Denmark. Since scaffolding work is cyclical, involving planning, construction, supervision, maintenance and assessment and dismantling, the more senior professionals are expected to be competent in solving problems and project management. In some countries, too, scaffolding construction workers are expected to work independently to a certain degree. It is safe to assume that the more differentiated the hierarchy of scaffolding occupation in each country, the less overall competence is expected of workers at the lower levels of competence, such as scaffolder and assistant scaffolder. Consequently, a higher level of cycle awareness and supervisory capability is required at the higher levels of the scaffolding occupation.

4.2 IVET and CVET in scaffolding

There are considerable differences between the countries investigated as to whether scaffolding training is confined to IVET, to CVET, or a mixture of both. Germany has the most comprehensive IVET system for scaffolding, stretching over three years and divided between the classroom, inter-company workshops, and site-based practical:
1. 13 weeks each year or a total of 39 weeks in the classroom
2. 10 weeks in the first and second years and 5 weeks in the third year
   in the inter-company workshops, totalling 25 weeks or 20% of the time
3. 20 weeks per year in the firm, totalling 60 weeks.

This comprehensive IVET system in Germany results in a recognised scaffolding qualification and was introduced initially for two years following the change from scaffolding being simply an activity carried out in the process of building to becoming a recognised occupation or *Beruf* in 1991. This contrasts with, for instance, UK where it was recognised as a skilled occupation in 1974, Poland, where it is still not recognised, and Finland, where there is almost no VET.

Where Germany also stands out is in having the career structure associated with other construction *Berufe*, as well as the possibility of becoming a *Meister* after three years of IVET plus 5 years of work experience, involving a CVET course of eight months full time, plus passing an exam. CVET for OSH is not obligatory and, though workers are repeatedly offered courses to keep up their competences, these are not well attended. OSH training too, whilst incorporated in IVET, has no predefined content in terms of CVET and workers do not anyway need to prove their OSH knowledge. For those

SCAFFOLD WORKSHOP 2:
VET IN THE SCAFFOLDING SECTOR

Hosted by Peter Kahl, Director,
Zeche Hansemann Training Centre,
Dortmund-Mengede, Germany,
13 February 2024

LINDA CLARKE
ProBE, University of Westminster

The focus of this workshop on training also seeks to ascertain the possibility of a European standard for OSH training for scaffolders, mindful that VET is a no-competence issue. Discussion revolved around the differences between different VET systems, such as:

- *Ireland*, 20 weeks off the job, over 2 years for the new apprenticeship, or certification obtained through the Construction Skills Certification Scheme (CSCS) in 17 days.
- *Netherlands*, where the main route is a certificate, no longer an apprenticeship, and trainees must be over 18 years old to work on heights, stretching over 20-25 days, though not all at once, as work experience time is required to progress to the next level.
- *Belgium*, where trainees are left free how to obtain certification, involving 20-25 days off-the-job training.
- *Germany*, 67 weeks off-the-job training over 3 years, 23 weeks a year, to EQF level 4.
- *UK*, 18 months-2 years training programme with 3 months off-the-job, in 2-week chunks.

Thus, the minimum off-the-job training period found is 3 weeks and the maximum 67 weeks, competence as a scaffolder varies considerably for different countries, and scaffolding training ranges from at one end formalised VET to simple certification and recognition through some training.

In terms of what is being learnt, training based on learning outcomes has no curriculum as such, though it is important to know what trainees are and should be learning. Mentoring is also important. There needs to be a minimum OSH training requirement, which, based on the certification schemes in Netherlands, Belgium, Ireland and UK, might be about 21 days. However, everything is to do with OSH, how to be safe on the scaffold, with extra training required for industrial scaffolding. How is it possible to separate OSH?

SCAFFOLD partners in the great hall

Trainee scaffolders project
Photos: Courtesy of Linda Clarke

without IVET, further training is possible through the social fund, and in this sense CVET is possible without IVET; the most qualified scaffolders are the most likely to update their qualifications, and vice versa.

Whilst the German VET system succeeds in attracting trainees, with 919 in 2022, the Dutch example provides a warning in that the IVET programme, which contained an on-the-job pathway as well as classroom-based training including, for instance, Dutch, maths and citizenship, is no longer offered because of lack of enrolment. Instead SVWOH (the Safe Working at Height Foundation) certification is preferred, established in 2016 to demonstrate professional competence, only for those over 18 years old, and consisting of courses to become an assistant scaffolder, a scaffolder, a chief scaffolder, scaffolding foreperson, a scaffolding inspector, and a supervisor of scaffolding in use respectively. There is, though, potentially, a lack of any further career structure and no specific or mandatory OSH certification for scaffolders. The Belgian system is in many respects similar to this, with very similar courses and without any necessary certification for scaffolders, though this may be required by employers. Poland too has no regulations specifying the length of training; basic training for scaffolding assembly and disassembly is instead incorporated into the formal education system as part of the practical VET within construction occupations, for instance bricklaying, as an additional qualification. Nevertheless, here OSH training is extensive and highly regulated.

In contrast to the demise of IVET in the Netherlands is scaffolding IVET in Ireland, which recently, in 2021, introduced a construction apprenticeship programme of two years. This includes on-the-job with an approved employer and off the job training at the National Construction Campus in the Scaffolding Apprenticeship Building to become a fully qualified scaffolder. In Ireland, formal training is a requirement for scaffolding, including OHS training, and the minimum standard of training required is certification under the Construction Skills Certification Scheme.

We see therefore considerable differences in both IVET and CVET in the different countries in relation to requirements, length, scope and how far IVET and CVET are merged. Most exemplary is probably Denmark, where IVET and CVET merge in its obligatory two-year industry training programme, which has some similarity to the new Irish scheme, though introduced much earlier, in 2009. The programme is for all scaffolders after three months or less of employment, on an alternating basis – that is off site in classroom or workshop and on site, on full salary (with a subsidy available), with different modules totalling 25 weeks overall, and according to the collective agreement. This includes a truck drivers' licence and crane and forklift certificates, whilst additional training is available for offshore work, including in OSH; indeed, an action plan is in place aimed at strengthening OSH training for scaffolders generally. The new 2023 collective agreement also has provision for training and upskilling if work is stopped, for instance, due to bad weather.

4.3. VET for scaffolding in different countries

As described above, scaffolding IVET and CVET programmes in the different countries vary considerably, not just in terms of content and structure but also the institutional arrangements in the different countries.

4.3.1. VET for scaffolding in Belgium

VET system

Belgian regulations state that workers using scaffolding, including those who assemble and dismantle scaffolding, must acquire the knowledge required to perform work at height by means of training. The employer must appoint and train competent persons, and training must also be provided for scaffold users. According to the Codex Welfare provisions, this training must cover:
*   measures to prevent the risks of persons or objects falling,
*   safety measures in the event of changing weather conditions that could impair the safety of the scaffolding concerned,
*   conditions relating to permissible loads.

The possible training courses for a scaffold user are:
o   basic safety, known as Safety Certification for Contractors or SCC ('SCC executives') and full safety SCC ('SCC supervisors'),
o   external training at a training centre, e.g. module 1 from *Constructiv*,
o   internal training (e.g. given by the supervisor/site manager).

Of importance here is that this training is traceable and considers regulatory requirements. Compared to internal training, with training at an external training centre it is easier to demonstrate (e.g. to the welfare inspectorate) that the requirements of the regulations have been met. To meet the knowledge and skills that scaffolders and scaffold users specifically need for their daily work, there are various training courses, all containing a theory component, whether supplemented by a practical component or not. The regulations themselves make no distinction between professional scaffolders and others but refer only to workers who assemble and dismantle scaffolding.

Based on the requirements of the legislation, *Constructiv* has developed a training programme, so-called modules 1, 2 and 3, which are included in its Code of Good Practice (https://www.buildingyourlearning.be/learningobject/4500/NL) (2023 Use and Assembly of Scaffolding). The main purpose of this code is to provide employers and employees with good practices, tips and examples of work and protective equipment that comply with the regulatory conditions and requirements associated with the use of scaffolding. The code is also a support and guide to apply the most appropriate way of working when assembling, dismantling, and changing the arrangement of scaffolding.

Purely in terms of regulation, Modules VWOH (safe working at height) 2 and 3 are sufficient as training unless the client requires scaffolders to be certified, whilst Module 1 is only for the use of scaffolding on site:

o   Working safely at height Module 2 – Scaffolding on site: For persons working on scaffolding and helping to assemble, dismantle or modify it.
o   Working safely at height Module 3 – Authorised person scaffolding on site.
    For persons responsible for erecting scaffolding, preparing calculation notes and checking correct erection.
o   Working at height safely Module mobile scaffolds (2 + 3) on site:
    For mobile scaffold users, mobile scaffold erectors and authorised persons on mobile scaffolds.

After attending a VWOH (Safely working at height) training course at a training centre, a document is drawn up attesting to attendance, which must be provided to each participant as soon as they have participated in the entire training cycle. In addition, for SCC-certified companies carrying out work in the petrochemical industry, specific requirements are imposed by clients (Bayer, etc.) and here training and a compulsory examination take place in a SCC-recognized centre. In addition, for Scaffolding construction, there are two training courses.
1.   AV-021: scaffolding builder
2.   AV-022: scaffolding inspector
There are equivalences here with modules 2 and 3.

Constructiv's person certification scheme is aligned with occupational competence profiles and a higher level than the above-mentioned courses (there are also exemptions possible for AV courses for those with a person certification). Though the regulations do not require certification of scaffolders, though this can be a requirement imposed by the client (e.g. in petrochemicals), at which point the requirement for certification becomes a contractual obligation.

OSH training

The law states that the employer shall ensure each employee receives sufficient and appropriate training related to their well-being in the performance of their work position. This training shall be adapted to the development of risks and the emergence of new risks and, if necessary, repeated at regular intervals.

Scaffolders do need to be in possession of a sectoral certificate that confirms specific competences and know-how after passing a theory test, whether this is supplemented by a practical test or not. A person's certificate is valid for 5 years and can be obtained after 'in-company' training, whose duration varies from company to company, or after training at an external training centre. OSH training is integrated into the VWOH training modules for scaffolders according to *Constructiv's* Professional Competence Profile and involves 3 days with exam (theory and practical) for the Assistant Scaffolder and 4 days each with exam (theoretical and practical) for the Scaffold builder, the Chief Scaffold builder, the Scaffolding Controller, and Scaffolding inspector.

Current and future developments

Working safely at height is a prerequisite, but far from a given. Together with the industry, *Constructiv* seeks to change this by improving the competence of employees involved in working at height. To this end, *Constructiv* manages certification schemes, final and test terms based on which employees can be trained and examined, and the central exam database and certificate register, CRC, where personal certificates related to safe working at height are stored. The objectives for the coming years are the further development of person certification for scaffolding in various languages and levels, striving for recognition of equivalence with training under the register of high-risk tasks (AV021 and AV022) and with the person certification scheme of the Netherlands (SVWOH certification scheme).

4.3.2. VET for scaffolding in Denmark

VET system

According to the collective agreement, an unskilled worker in the scaffolding sector must after three months employment be offered training as a scaffolding fitter through an industry training programme that consists of practical and theoretical parts. Apprentices receive a full salary from the employer, who can apply for a subsidy to finance it. Previously, the requirement was various courses for experienced scaffolding workers in the industry and not an actual training programme. In 1992, however, the social partners established the two-year training contract programme for scaffolders and in 1997, a statutory requirement for a minimum 3-weeks training in system scaffolding was introduced. From then on, the sector was in no doubt that all professional scaffolding workers should be trained. In renewing the collective agreement in 2009, the parties accordingly agreed that the two-year scaffolding training should be mandatory for all new employees. Since then, the sector has been developing the programme, recognising the need for a well-educated workforce. The programme is developed and financed jointly by the union, 3F *Fagligt Fælles Forbund,* and the Danish Construction Industry Association's Scaffolding Section. The social partners focus on having a qualified labour force in the construction industry and 3F *Byggegruppen* has always worked strategically to ensure education and training for its members and, thus, also for scaffolding workers.

The first three months of employment in the scaffolding sector are a probationary period, which can be cancelled unilaterally. The two-year scaffolding fitter programme is then structured so that workers alternate between attending courses organised in modules at the training centre, totalling approximately 25 weeks or 120 days, including obtaining certificates for all completed courses and a truck driving licence, and working in the company with which they have a training contract. Once the apprentice has completed all courses, a final examination is held, which results in certification as a scaffolder. The VET programme provides insight into the working environment and consists of several OSH training programmes that aim to ensure that workers have completed a training programme or passed a test before they are allowed to perform work that can cause a significant accident risk or health hazard. Training requirements cannot be waived so that work is not simply carried out under the "instructions" of a site manager or similar, but rather the individual's educational qualifications are decisive.

These requirements for the educational elements, as described in the "Operational procedure on Occupational Health and Safety Education", also apply to workers coming from outside Denmark, who must meet them to have their competencies in scaffolding assembly recognised to work in the sector. There are also specific qualification requirements for small-scale scaffolding used by other construction professionals, so that different levels of training are necessary for all types of scaffolding. The survey conducted under the 2019 *Action Plan 3* to identify scaffolding workers in the sector showed that around 51% of participants had completed the entire two-year scaffolder training programme, while around 27%, including, for example, apprentices, had undertaken individual scaffolding modules.

Training content

The scaffolding fitter programme provides competencies to erect, cover and secure scaffolding, including how to plan complex scaffolding tasks that require strength and stability calculations. The programme provides an in-depth insight into:
- How to cordon off and signpost the site before work begins
- What loads the scaffolding must be able to withstand and how it is secured
- How height, surface, roofing and weather conditions affect stability calculations.

In addition to scaffolding knowledge, general skills such as customer service, co-operation and understanding drawings are acquired. The programme works, in particular, with system scaffolding, pipe and coupling scaffolding, setting up special scaffolding, enclosure and total enclosure scaffolding, and coordinated scaffolding assembly. Furthermore, it is mandatory to obtain the necessary licences to drive forklifts, work with cranes and comply with the safety requirements for working on roads.

OSH training

OSH for scaffolders is integrated into the scaffolder training programme. The programme provides insight into the working environment in the industry and includes OSH training programmes aiming to ensure that on completion or having passed a test a person is allowed to perform work that may cause a significant risk of accidents or health hazard. Scaffold-related working environment and safety are included under rescue from heights; there is also statutory overall working environment and safety training for Working Environment Representatives.

Current and future developments

The 2023 collective agreement introduced provisions to consider the possibilities for further training and upskilling in the event of work stoppages and being sent home due to weather and other conditions, as well as for employees to appoint a training manager in individual companies to focus on training and further training. The agreement also creates an incentive to include apprentices in the pricing of on-the-job training, consisting of trained scaffolders receiving a so-called "mentor supplement" for taking on apprentices. This is intended to motivate more scaffolders to take on apprentices to retain apprentices in training and obtain more trained scaffolders, as well as strengthening the sector in the long term. The parties in the scaffolding sector work together to ensure retention but the average scaffolder stays for only 11 years. Those who stay tend to have completed the programme, but many do not complete the entire scaffolder training programme because they leave the industry; there is a high turnover rate. The programme is continuously being modernised to adapt to developments, including new materials, technological developments, health and safety requirements, etc.

4.3.3. VET for scaffolding in Germany

VET system

Scaffolding VET is part of what is known as the 'dual system', divided between state and industry, and thus leads to a vocational qualification recognised throughout the entire national system of education and employment. Whilst training as a scaffolder has had the status of a recognised training occupation or *Beruf* with a two-year programme since 1991, only since 1998, has scaffolding been considered a full *Beruf*, for which a three-year VET programme (practical and workshop training in the company, theoretical training in the vocational school) is required. This training can be supplemented and continued by a systematic further training career up to the level of scaffolding master or *Meister*. The status as a recognised vocational qualification is important in professional life, above all for classification according to collective agreements, but also at the beginning when applying for a job. It may also be required for admission to further education and training; for example, the *Meister* examination and courses preparing for this are usually linked to a completed IVET programme, as, under certain circumstances, is entry to higher education studies. IVET usually begins after graduation from general school education, at the age of 16, though in scaffolding more than half of the VET entrants are already at least 18 years old and one in six is over 24 years. Most trainees come with a certificate from a lower secondary school, and a small, but growing, number has a university entrance qualification; only a few are women.

Inter-company training: In scaffolding, as for other construction occupations, part of the practical training takes place in inter-company training centres, which play an important role as many small companies cannot cover the entire breadth of an occupation's activities and do not always have the wide range of modern technical equipment needed. The training centres, in contrast, paid for by a training levy of 2.1 % of companies' gross wage bill, are at the cutting edge of technical and vocational pedagogical development. The three training locations (company, vocational school and inter-company training centre) are obliged to coordinate their different training content.

Attractiveness of vocational training in scaffolding

Detailed data on trainee numbers over time are published regularly by the Federal Institute for Vocational Education and Training (BIBB) and on the participation of companies of different sizes in training by SOKA *Gerüstbau*. According to the SOKA data, there were 919 trainees in 2022, over all three training years, whilst BIBB structural data indicate that, of all trainees in 2021, 16 % were of non-German nationality. Over time, BIBB data reveal significant changes: in 1998, 423 young people began scaffolding but numbers each year then fell to 279 in 2006, rising again two years later to 438, declining to 345 in 2018 and then increasing to 393 in 2021.

BIBB data on the school-leaving qualifications of those entering scaffolding training show that in 2021 just under 50 % of those starting training are from the lower achieving *Hauptschule* and about 25 % from the higher level *Realschule*, whilst just under 14 % had not completed lower secondary school, and 9 % had a higher education entrance qualification. VET participation differs markedly according to the size of the company, with small and very small companies (with fewer than ten employees) accounting for more than half of all companies in 2022 (56 %) but offering under 22 % of training places, whilst large firms (with 50 or more employees), comprising only 2 % of all firms account for about 20 % of all training places. Successful completion numbers are, however, very much lower than those for entrants, fluctuating between 150 and 200 per year till 2021, apart from 2013 at 240, but since then numbering less than 100, whilst the examination success rate was about two-thirds. Successful examination participation by women has been sporadic and only in a few years.

A general problem of VET for scaffolding is the premature termination of contracts, not including those cases where the training company changes but the scaffolding training continues. Though there has a slight reduction in the number of prematurely terminated training contracts in scaffolding over the last five years, from over 50 % to 40 %, this rate remains high and a vocational pedagogical challenge.

VISIT TO *ZECHE HANSEMANN* SCAFFOLDING TRAINING CENTRE

Hosted by Director Peter Kahl,
Dortmund-Mengede, Germany,
December 2023 and February 2024

LINDA CLARKE
ProBE, University of Westminster

The centre was set up in 1997, the same year scaffolding was recognised as a full *Handwerk*, and is the only such centre in Europe and the most advanced scaffolding centre in the world, covering the whole of the scaffolding sector up to *Meister* level, The site was developed as a coal mine in 1870, which was closed in the 1960s, and in 1991 rescued for scaffolding training by obtaining public funds. There are three training centres for scaffolding in Germany, including *Zeche Hansemann*, serving North-West Germany up to the Dutch border and stretching to East Germany, and another in Magdeburg covering also Berlin. The Centre seeks to be foremost in terms of scaffolding, working with Dortmund and Bochum universities, for instance on digitalisation, as well as with manufacturers and companies.

The training is for 3 years maximum (those with a *Fachabitur* can shorten the training), including in the *Berufschule*, also situated in the centre, which covers subjects such as physics and maths. Each year trainees spend 13 weeks in the *Berufschule*, 10 in the training centre, and 20 in the firm, totalling 23 weeks off the job, in 4-week blocks, plus 6 weeks holiday. There is also Boarding House accommodation, which opened in 1999, with 26 rooms for guests and 220 beds for the trainees. There are 400 trainees attending, over 3 years, ranging from 16-35 years, both men and two women; 65% of those training are of non-German origin and 40% are migrants, including from Turkey and Morocco. The training

Scaffolding for bridge construction

Hanging scaffold

ranges from the simple scaffolding for a single house to a hanging scaffold to planning a façade, covering all types of scaffolding, including tube and fittings, regarded as the 'mother of all scaffolds', at the beginning, so that trainees learn the basis of the occupation. After 2 years training, trainees can make a scaffold plan themselves in the *Berufschule* as it is important for employers to have a qualified person to carry out the planning, using complex software. Trainees must be properly equipped, and their health and safety are paramount; they also receive physical and sports training. The weight limit is, for instance, a maximum 20 kilos and a higher-level guard rail is always used. There are 9 *Meisters* on site.

The Centre has a continuing VET (CVET) programme, produced in consultation with the social partners, including the union *IG Bau*. This includes, for instance, train the trainers funded by the social fund and 10 days training after 2 years' experience, as well as a 6-week training course to be a team leader/ganger. In scaffolding there is a 3-person hierarchy, from unskilled (*ungelernte*) to *Monteur*, *Montageleiter*, and *Kolonnenführer*. There is also an 8-month *Meister* course, full- or part-time, covering practical, theoretical, commercial, and training aspects, with a Germany-wide catchment area. The course is in four parts, the first two each involving an 8-hour exam and parts 3 and 4 each 2 day-exams, at a total cost, including travel and accommodation, of € 30,000, for which grants or a loan can be obtained.

Scaffolding is becoming lighter, though tolerances are better with traditional, now seldom used as system/modular scaffolding is flexible and quicker. The Centre has 2,000 tons of material, 18,000 metres of pipes, 9,600 metres of planks, and 14,000 square metres of space outside. It has a wide range of equipment, covering many systems, which means maintaining important relations with manufacturers. There is a heavy loads area, with 4 different types of load-bearing equipment, according to whether the trainees are first or second year or more experienced. Everywhere too are rescue huts.

Tube and fittings: the mother of all scaffolds

Scaffolding VET curriculum

VET content covers the entire range of work required in the scaffolding construction cycle, from preparatory surveying work, setting up a construction site and assessing load-bearing foundations, to establishing the load-bearing capacity, the materials to be used and the various common work processes and work techniques, to the handling and maintenance of tools, equipment, machines and technical facilities required for this, including:
- the maintenance, storage and transport of scaffolding components,
- the anchoring of scaffolding,
- the construction of length- and area-oriented working and protective scaffolds,
- the construction of shoring with substructure including the basic formwork,
- knowledge and use of working platforms, working platforms and lifts,
- the construction of suspended scaffolding,
- the construction of weather protection halls and enclosures, and
- the construction of scaffolding for special requirements.

Furthermore, quality assurance measures and reporting are part of the IVET programme, as well as OHS measures and environmental protection.

Further education

In the scaffolding *Beruf*, additional training opportunities are established by the framework collective agreement of 2015 and financed by the social fund for scaffolding (SOKA *Gerüstbau*). This further training path is primarily aimed at persons entering professional work without a basic initial education and training *("Quereinsteiger")* and offers the possibility of advancing from unskilled work to the position of a worker in qualified professional functions on the construction site on the basis of professional experience, through learning in the process of work and through supplementary courses. These advanced training levels are referred to as:
o *Geprüfter Gerüstbaumonteur* (Certified Scaffolding Assembler)
o *Geprüfter Gerüstbaumontageleiter* (Certified Scaffolding Erection Supervisor), with basic knowledge of quantity surveying and normally leading and controlling a group of workers
o *Geprüfter Gerüstbaukolonnenführer* (Certified Scaffolding Crew Leader), with more advanced knowledge and leading and controlling several groups, up to leading scaffolding work on an entire site.

In 2021 there were 53 registered for the *Geprüfte Gerüstbaukolonnenführer* examinations, all men. Those participating are admitted to preparation courses of several weeks, having proved a certain period of professional activity on a construction site in the respective previous function. SOKA *Gerüstbau* is obliged to finance participation according to the collective agreement, so long as the preparatory courses do not fall short of a certain minimum duration or if regular attendance cannot be proven. In addition, a *Quereinsteiger* (career changer) can use a comparable CVET pathway to catch up on their participation in the final third year IVET examination to become a recognised skilled scaffolder.

For a professional career in scaffolding, there is the possibility since 2001 to complete further training to become a *Meister* based on completed VET and subsequent relevant professional practice of at least five years. The scaffolding *Meister* examinations are regulated through the *Handwerk* Code and passes have since 2001 averaged 65 per year, standing at 76 in 2022.

OSH training

OSH training is part of the occupational profile to which VET for scaffolders is geared. The regulation, which describes the abilities or competencies to be demonstrated in the final examination at the end of the third year, explicitly states that 'occupational health and safety measures' must be realised in executing the practical examination task. Knowledge acquisition has been facilitated by standardising the scaffolding of all manufacturers so that workers do not have to deal with the peculiarities of different scaffolding systems.

Scaffolders are regularly offered training courses lasting a few days each, which enable them to keep their competencies in the field of OSH constantly up to date. These courses are offered by *BG Bau* and various other further educational institutions. *BG Bau*-run training courses make workers aware of dangers and risks in the workplace, the importance of their own responsibility and initiative, and the possible consequences of careless behaviour, whilst companies are informed about the material consequences of a lack of OSH and can receive premiums for preventing accidents. *BG Bau* also provides information on assembling protective devices, working procedures, how to behave safely on various types of scaffolding and mobile working platforms, the correct use of lifts, the use of edge protection on construction sites, such as side protection and barriers, as well as safety nets and safety scaffolds, and roof safety scaffolds. However, the courses are not subject to any predefined rules, their content and scope as well as timing and frequency of participation is for employees to choose. They are voluntary and there is no obligation to attend events and regularly prove that OSH knowledge required has been acquired. The decision on this is ultimately the responsibility of the contractor. Those who already have good prerequisites generally update their level of knowledge continuously through CVET, which means that those companies and their employees in which OSH enjoys a high priority regularly participate in OSH training, whilst a low level of knowledge and of efforts in the field of OSH coincides with low participation.

The importance of OSH in view of the hazards of working at height is reflected, among other things, in the existence of OSH officers who work within the individual company or are engaged by scaffolding companies as external service providers. These officers must complete a special training course, comprising four courses of six weeks each within two years. In addition, theoretical learning units must be completed, either online at home or in the company and regular refresher training is recommended but

THE DEVELOPMENT OF VOCATIONAL TRAINING FOR SCAFFOLDERS IN GERMANY

FRANK KROLLE
Director of Studies, *Fritz-Henßler-Berufskolleg*
of the City of Dortmund

In Germany, the "dual vocational training system" has been established and successful since the end of the 1960s. The "dual system" refers to the two vocational education partners of the trainee: the privately organised training company focusing on operational requirements and the imparting of practical knowledge and, on the other hand, the state-organised vocational school in which theoretical knowledge is imparted. Every year, almost 500,000 young people in Germany are successfully trained in their profession through this system. At present, dual training is uniformly regulated in this way in over 300 different vocational occupations or *Berufe* in Germany.

Scaffolding was denied recognition as a 'recognised *Beruf*' until the 1990s. Scaffolders had either completed other training courses or were precariously employed as 'casual workers.' Increasing demands regarding technology and safety led to training as a full *Beruf* (since 1998), with 3 years of regulated training being the mandatory standard in Germany. Since then, training for scaffolders has taken place in regional companies and in three interconnected training and education centres. The advantage of this training system for both training partners is evident in its ability to react flexibly to changing market requirements and technical developments. Harmonisation in the European context could be a challenge for this form of training, but due to the flexibility of the dual system, it is not a cause for concern but is rather highly welcome.

not obligatory. One of the tasks of the OSH officer is risk assessment, which is mandatory and refers to an expert person examining the site and work involved at the beginning of site set-up to determine where possible sources of danger exist and how they can be countered. However, in the case of simple, small construction sites planned for a short period, the risk assessment is often either not carried out or not thorough enough.

4.3.4. VET for scaffolding in Ireland

Forms of apprenticeships

The national apprenticeship system is governed by legislation, principally the 1967 Industrial Training Act, which sets out the overall structure and protections for and responsibilities of apprentices, employers and VET providers. Apprenticeship is defined as a structured VET programme formally combining and alternating learning in the workplace with learning in an education or training centre. It is a blended combination of on-the-job employer-based training and off-the-job VET programmes, delivered by further education providers. These lead to awards from EQF (European Qualification Framework) levels 2-5 (Irish National Framework of Qualifications (NFQ) levels 3-6), with some higher apprenticeships at EQF level 6 (NFQ levels 7-8), the levels also being used as a recruitment tool (QQI, 2023). The state agency responsible for external quality assurance is Quality and Qualifications Ireland (QQI), which validates programmes, make awards and is responsible for the promotion, maintenance, development and review of NFQ (QQI, 2023). The 2012 Quality Assurance Act also underpins apprenticeship, supporting national validation and quality assurance arrangements for programmes. If a qualification was obtained outside Ireland, the National Academic Recognition Information Centre (NARIC) advises on how it is understood.

The main VET providers are 16 education and training boards (ETBs), whilst SOLAS is the government agency responsible for funding, planning and coordinating VET, including maintenance of registers of approved employers and of apprentices (Cedefop, 2021, 2022). The duration of the traditional construction craft apprenticeships is over four years and the new consortia-led apprenticeships between 2 and 4 years, though these must also provide progression pathways to higher education. The National Apprenticeship Council is responsible for overseeing and implementing the consortia-led Construction Apprenticeship programme, which since 2021 includes scaffolding. This two-year practical scaffolding programme has eight modules, developed in consultation with industry, and includes on-the-job training with a SOLAS-approved employer and off-the-job training in the National Construction Campus purpose-built Scaffolding Apprenticeship Building. The Scaffolding apprenticeship is managed by Laois and Offaly ETB, and, on completion, participants become a fully qualified scaffolder, with a QQI Level 5 Certificate in Scaffolding.

Formal training, which includes instruction on any risks involved, is required for those who erect, add to, alter, or dismantle a scaffold. The extent of training required depends on the type of work normally undertaken and the type of scaffold. The minimum acceptable standard of training is the approved Construction Skills Certification Scheme (CSCS) for Basic Scaffolders, or an equivalent training programme accredited by SOLAS. Through CSCS, SOLAS assesses scaffolders, issues cards, and keeps a register of certified scaffolders. On successful completion of the initial training and CSCS assessment, scaffolders should keep a record of their subsequent work experience (HSA, 2018).

A competent worker/person is defined in the 2005 Safety Health and Welfare at Work Act as someone who 'possess sufficient training, experience and knowledge appropriate to the nature of the work to be undertaken'. Scaffolding activities beyond the range of general access scaffolds require erectors to be trained to an advanced level. Employers, contractors and project supervisors for the construction process should ensure that those erecting scaffolding have the necessary training and competence by seeking evidence of QQI certification or an equivalent SOLAS-accredited qualification. Anybody with qualifications and training from another EU Member State can apply to SOLAS for recognition of their training under EU (Recognition of Professional Qualifications) Regulations 2017 (S.I. 8 of 2017) and, if deemed equivalent, be issued with a SOLAS CSCS card of the appropriate level (temporary services card or experienced operator's card) (HSA, 2018).

Two systems for the training/assessment of scaffolders are thus in place: CSCS, with basic (7 days) and advanced (10 days) off-the job training and assessment programmes, delivered by a SOLAS Approved Training Organisation (ATO); and the new two-year apprenticeship, involving 20 weeks off-the -job training, delivered by Laois/Offaly ETB at the National Construction Campus. A consortium consisting of training providers, unions and employers developed the scaffolding apprenticeship and the first graduates qualified from this programme in late 2023 (Carey, 2023).

OSH training

Statutory OSH training is required by law or deemed necessary through risk and/or organisational needs assessment, so helping to ensure the safety, health and welfare of employees and others who may be affected by work activities. OSH training for scaffolders includes:
- *SafePass,* a mandatory one-day OHS awareness programme, repeated every 4 years, aiming to raise the standard of safety awareness in the construction industry and secure that, over time, all site personnel have undergone basic training to enable them to work onsite without being a risk to themselves or others who might be affected by their acts or omissions. Candidates successfully completing the programme receive a SafePass Registration Card.
- *Manual Handling,* a half-day course, repeated every 3 years, which provides the knowledge and skills to correctly pre-assess, lift, carry and lower objects and identifies best health and safety practice (Safetech, 2023).
- *Working At Height*, a half-day course, repeated every 3 years, designed for all personnel who work at height, aiming to increase awareness of the hazards and risks involved, and also designed for people who may be required to rescue a person from a height.

Current and future developments

SOLAS in partnership with SIPTU, Ireland's largest union, and the National Association of Scaffolding and Access Contractors (NASAC) are continuously striving for a safe environment for workers. Amendments to scaffolding programmes were finalised before January 2017 when the Scaffolding CSCS training programmes were updated, changing routes of entry and experience required before attending a CSCS programme. The Code of Practice on Access and Working Scaffold was updated in 2018 by the HSA in consultation with the social partners. In 2021 the Laois Offaly ETB introduced the new scaffolding apprenticeship with the support of NASAC and SIPTU. It is envisaged that the scaffolding apprenticeship will replace the CSCS method of training scaffolders in-whole or in-part at some stage in the future. Accordingly, delivering scaffolding training through a recognised level 5 apprenticeship model is an important step forward and means that there is an accredited qualification for those working in this area, so helping with their career progression pathways.

The Construction Safety Licensing Bill will see new arrangements introduced for many activities and, though scaffolding is not currently a scheduled activity, the aim is to further improve OSH in the construction industry, in which scaffolders play a prominent role. The Bill makes provisions for the list of activities to be reviewed so that at a future point this may include scaffolders who have completed their apprenticeship (Milley, 2023).

The role of the social partners in VET

The union movement understands that the value of accredited training programmes across the construction industry's myriad occupations cannot be overstated, ensuring that those whose responsibility is to erect, alter or dismantle a scaffold have had their knowledge, skills and competencies evaluated to a specified standard. This also ensures the workers involved in the industry can follow an educational pathway that may not otherwise have been open to them. Returning to education through accredited skills-based occupational training and achieving a further or higher education award can lead workers toward a lifelong learning journey, promoting ongoing personal development and educational attainment that allows them to reach their full potential in their chosen field and provides the sector with highly skilled, competent and motivated people (Gallagher, 2023).

The Construction Industry Federation (CIF), the representative employer body for contractors working in the construction industry, recognises that to deliver projects safely and on budget and to meet client specification, having a skilled and well-trained workforce is vital. To be a sustainable industry, too, CIF recognises that to attract young people to work in the sector, pathways to entry and continual upskilling need to be offered. To this end, CIF and its members are committed to training and continual professional development (CPD) in the sector, as demonstrated by engagement in:
-   Construction Industry Register of Ireland (CIRI), designed to drive competency through training and CPD,
-   IVET and CVET programmes for the sector meeting industry requirements,
-   Construction Safety Partnership Advisory Committee (CSPAC), whose 2000 Action Plan commits to making scaffolding training mandatory under the Construction Regulations (derived from the Mobile Sites Directive).

4.3.5. VET for scaffolding in the Netherlands

VET system

There are three options for ensuring that professional competence is objectively demonstrable through the structure of the VET system:
1. VET diploma, issued on behalf of the government by the educational institution,
2. Recognition of Competencies Acquired Elsewhere (*Erkenning van Verworven Competenties* – EVC) professional competence diploma, issued by EVC Expertise Centre
3. Certificate according to ISO 17024 (personal certificate), issued on behalf of *Stichting Veilig Werken Op Hoogte* (Safe Working at Height Foundation) by a recognised certification body.

Within the VET system, there is a Scaffolding qualification dossier for Scaffolders and Chief Scaffolders, involving programmes with a 'training on the job pathway', whereby trainees both work and study. No training has been provided in either programme for several years due to lack of enrolment so that educational institutions no longer offer them. As well as vocational skills, the VET course includes subjects such as Dutch, maths and citizenship, making the duration longer than that needed for personal certification. Given the market demand for scaffolders, a short process via personal certification provides an alternative, especially as many employees come from non-Dutch-speaking countries and are therefore adults, which means that IVET is inappropriate. The disappearance of those in receipt of VET is of concern as many permanent employees working in the sector have been through the VET system and form a group operating at the levels of Scaffolder and Chief Scaffolder. The current middle management in scaffolding is also made up of those who have completed the VET scaffolding programme and developed based on this solid foundation. The disappearance of the VET programme may mean that in the long-term companies have difficulties finding people able to progress to executive positions.

Personal certification

Professional competence is demonstrated, monitored and registered manner through the Scaffolding Guideline, which sets out the training structure for working safely at height (scaffolding) applying to the Assistant Scaffolder, Scaffolder and Chief Scaffolder profiles. The Guideline includes mandatory personal certification to ensure that the expertise and skills regarding safety, applications of technical activities, knowledge of legal provisions, etc., of those involved remain at a professional level. Since January 2017, this structure has been part of the *Stichting Veilig Werken Op Hoogte* (Safe Working at Height Foundation – SVWOH), established in 2016 on the initiative of the Association of Scaffolding, Height Working and Concrete Formwork Companies (VSB) and *Bouwend Nederland* KOMAT. SVWOH is made up of scaffolding companies, clients (e.g. Shell and ENGIE), construction companies, and unions and was set up to promote safe working at height and to demonstrate the professional competence and expertise of personnel directly or indirectly involved daily in assembling and providing a safe temporary workplace for working at height, as in scaffolding.

The Foundation's activities include:
- Setting up, maintaining, managing and facilitating the Central Examination Bank for Safe Working at Height,
- Registration in the SSVV Central Diploma Register (shared management),
- Certification of individuals, final attainment and assessment targets for professional competence profiles,
- The Board of Experts, Examination Committee and the 'Work Chambers' (specialised sections),
- Information provision and knowledge transfer,
- Collaboration with certifying bodies.

Content and assessment experts on the SVWOH Examination Committee, which works to ensure high-quality certification schemes and exams, represent industry associations, clients and contractors in scaffolding. A system of different working groups and committees has been set up for this collaborative work and, in this way, SVWOH ensures the quality of the personal certification process in accordance with the ISO-17024 standard.

After each five-year certification period, a new determination must be made that the certificate holder meets the requirements of the certification scheme (recertification). The certifying body (DNV) is responsible for issuing a personal certificate but may outsource examination and assessment work to an examination organisation, with which it enters into an agreement, and which may in turn also enter into an agreement with SVWOH, which issues the exams. Certification takes place once it has been demonstrated that the professional competence requirements based on the examination regulations and the certification scheme have been met.

Types of certificates

The scaffolding sector has the following certificates in accordance with the Scaffolding Guideline:
- *Assistant Scaffolder:* assists with assembly and dismantling work but is not yet allowed to assemble or dismantle scaffolds independently. If an assistant scaffolder assists with assembly work, this must only be of simple category 1 scaffolds, under the supervision of either the scaffolder, the chief scaffolder or the foreperson.
- *Scaffolder:* independently assembles and dismantles simple category 1 scaffolds and may assemble complex scaffolds under the supervision of someone at least chief scaffolder level.

VISIT TO A VSB SCAFFOLDING TRAINING CENTRE, THE NETHERLANDS

Hosted by Gerard Westenbroek
(Industry Manager, Dutch Scaffolding Association (VSB)
and Emile Bakkum (Director of STE Training Centre),
May 2023

LINDA CLARKE

ProBE, University of Westminster

In the Netherlands, scaffolding became a sector from the 1970s, though earlier in industry. The VSB *(Vereiniging van Steiger – Hoogwerk – en Betonbekistingbedrijven)* centre was founded in 1992 and trains for all industry, including offshore (e.g. hanging scaffold), housing, construction (new build, renovation), and shipyards. There are 4 grades of scaffolders, from unskilled to semi-skilled to skilled, and scaffolders usually work in threes as a team. The most serious accidents are falling from heights, either of users or scaffolders, though scaffolders only rarely fall from heights. Companies pay for the training. The small scaffolding companies are more stable and large ones bring dozens of scaffolders for training; agency labour also comes through the centre. The main courses are:

Assistant Scaffolding (4 days + 1 day exam),
Basic Scaffolding (3 days + 1 day exam),
Advanced Scaffolding (4 days + 1 day exam),
Foreperson Scaffolding (6 days + 3-hour exam),
Scaffolding Inspector (4 days + 2.5-hour exam),
Safety Assessment Level 1 (1 day + 30-minute exam), and
Safety Assessment Level 2 (3 days plus 2-hour exam).

Exams are digital, cover both theory and practical, and are conducted in different languages, including German and English as well as Dutch. At the time of the visit there were 22 trainees from different countries and 4 trainers.

The centre is well-equipped, both inside, where there are scaffolding mockups plus a range of parts as well as PPE, and outside in the yard. For the past 35-40 years systems scaffolding is the most used in the industry, though basic or traditional scaffolding (as in UK) is also used, especially on smaller projects. Scaffolding is very durable, and components are now lighter and stronger.

- *Chief Scaffolder:* independently assembles and dismantles simple and complex scaffolds and is entitled to independently deliver scaffolds up to and including category 3.
- *Scaffolding Foreperson:* performs the same scaffolding technical actions as the chief scaffolder and has additional competencies regarding scaffolding inspection, and leadership, communication, management and administrative skills. The foreperson is entitled to independently deliver scaffolds up to and including category 3 and scaffolds of category 4 in the presence of the designer.
- *Scaffolding Inspector:* deals with the inspection and clearance of scaffolds and must be able to assess the safety of the constructed scaffold, a function primarily involving engagement with the client, or the party in the chain to which the scaffold has been formally transferred.
- *Scaffolding Use Supervisor:* must be able to assess the safety of the constructed scaffolds, both standard and complex configurations (categories 1, 2, 3 and 4). The Supervisor communicates at the technical level of the chief scaffolder or the foreperson. To demonstrate ability to carry out the work at the desired level, this officer must hold the Scaffolding Use Supervisor certificate.

In addition to these job levels, a position on intake has been included in recent years, namely Aspiring Assistant Scaffolder, who does not assemble or dismantle. The entrance criteria for the registered aspiring assistant scaffolder are:

a. Must be at least 18 years old,
b. Must hold a valid Dutch VCA certificate at the outset,
c. Must register with the SVWOH,
d. After no more than one year, must hold the Assistant Scaffolder personal certificate and be registered in the Central Diploma Register (CDR) otherwise he/she will be deregistered from the SVWOH and can no longer work in the position.

Training content

The training programme for scaffolders has a nominal length of two years and that for chief scaffolders a nominal length of three years. A personal certificate may be obtained by taking training programmes/courses with commercial training providers, in combination with relevant practical experience and concluded by an independent examination by one of the examination agencies recognised by the certifying body. The length of these training programmes/courses varies depending on the training provider. In addition, the large scaffolding companies often provide specialised training to employees, including training for specific scaffolds, though such courses have no formal status. Ergonomics is part of the curriculum and the exam in VET and personal certification courses.

OSH training

OSH training is in place for all workers in the construction industry, not specific for scaffolders. To be allowed to work as a scaffolder, the person must have demonstrable expertise by being in possession of a VCA (*Veiligheids Checklist Aannemers* or Safety, Health and Environment Checklist Contractors / SCC) certificate and a personal certificate in scaffolding.

Current and future developments

In recent years, personal certification has taken over the role of the IVET programme regarding preparation for safe and expert work and has increased the quality of workers in scaffolding. The Scaffolding Guideline is currently being revised and once adopted final attainment and assessment targets of all personal certificates will be revised in line and the Aspiring Assistant Scaffolder personal certificate will no longer apply as the entry level position will be Assistant Scaffolder.

4.3.6. VET for scaffolding in Poland

VET system

Basic information on the use of scaffolding and related requirements (mainly regarding work safety) are integrated into the formal VET system (trade school) and enshrined in the core curriculum of all basic qualifications / construction professions at EQF levels 3-4 Polish Qualifications Framework. This training element is included not as an autonomous element but as part of practical VET within the units of a given occupation. Apprenticeship is not the dominant form in the VET system.

Scaffolding installer training is thus not included in the formal VET system taking place in trade schools but takes place in training centres in a non-formal system. The price of a course to become a scaffolding assembler in 2021 ranged from around PLN 1,000 (€ 235) to PLN 2,000 (€ 470), though since then there has been a significant price increase due to inflation. The key to training is to prepare the candidate to pass the qualification exam (cost PLN 350 or € 82) before a commission appointed by the Łukasiewicz Network Institute of Technology in Warsaw and to obtain an entry in the assembler / operator's book, confirming the licence to assemble scaffolding, and in the register kept by the Operators Training Centre of the Warsaw Institute. Currently, entry in the register is made for an indefinite period and there is no obligation to renew the licence. Certificates of completion of the course issued by training centres that train scaffolding users and supervise scaffolding installation are only informative for the worker concerned and the employer. Companies providing OSH training (periodic and job-related) for assemblers and users also keep records of those trained.

Training content

There are no regulations specifying the length of scaffolding installer training though most training centres allocate between 80 and 100 hours (theoretical and practical training). The Warsaw Institute of Technology recommends a scaffolding assembler training programme to training centres but does not enforce its implementation.

OSH training

OSH Training for scaffolders is an integral part of the training required to become a certified scaffolder and is divided into initial training – general and on-the-job – and periodic. Companies providing scaffolding installation services carry out additional specialised OSH training, depending on the system used. According to current legislation, OSH training is carried out prior to the admission to work, but after the conclusion of the employment contract, which means that the initial OSH training cannot be carried out prior to the conclusion of the employee's contract. Information as well as practical guidance is provided to the scaffolder candidate during the training course before the examination.

OSH requirements for scaffolding construction are the basis for allowing workers to both erect and use scaffolding and are the most detailed part of the scaffolding regulations, including basic regulations for the correct installation of scaffolding, which must be included in the training. These define the rules for the construction of the scaffold structure and platform:

- *Its structure* must be stable and protected against toppling by braces or anchors and not extend more than 3 m above the last line of anchors.
- *The platform* itself should be solid, secured against displacement and surrounded by protective barriers.
- *All external sides* should be surrounded by a protective railing at a height of 1.1 m (or 1 m for system scaffolding) and be provided with a 0.15 m high kerb and an intermediate railing.
- *There must be a balustrade* on the inside (if the scaffolding is set back more than 0.2 m from the building). If an internal balustrade cannot be used, the platform must be widened by using consoles.
- *The uppermost platform* may extend a maximum of 1.5 m above the last anchor line.
- *Walkway platforms* must have lockable manholes.
- *Their working area* must be large enough to accommodate workers, and to store tools and necessary materials.
- *The communication risers* on the scaffolding must not be more than 20 m away from the workstation.
- *When a so-called "Warsaw scaffold" is used*, it is important to supplement the scaffold frames with extensions up to a height of 1.1 m, as the height of the standard frames of this type of scaffold is not sufficient to protect against falls from height.

- *After strong winds,* precipitation and work interruptions lasting more than 10 days, the scaffolding should be inspected by the site manager or another person with building qualifications.
- Apart from these cases, *a periodic inspection* at least once a month is necessary. The method for carrying out the inspection is described in the manufacturer's instructions or in the individual project.

All these elements must be included in the health and safety training of the scaffolder and the scaffold user. In addition:

o Training must cover the use of personal protective equipment, permissible loads (loads to be carried/lifted by the worker).
o The scaffold may only be accessed using the ladders provided for this purpose on the inside.
o Never climb the scaffolding from the outside.
o It is also forbidden to climb on guard rails, to leave materials on platforms after work is completed and to carry people on mobile scaffolding, which may only be accessed if the brakes are on at least two diagonal wheels.
o Working on, and erecting and dismantling scaffolding is prohibited in unfavourable conditions such as lack of adequate lighting after dark, dense fog, rain or snowfall, glare, thunderstorms or strong winds in excess of 10 m/s (c38 km/h).
o The training course shall be supplemented by provisions on measures.

OSH training for scaffolders is an integral part of the training required to become a certified scaffolder. The prerequisite for admission to the scaffolder course is:

1. A current medical certificate issued to the candidate, certifying that there are no health objections to the occupation of scaffolder,
2. Completion of training in the M-BHP- OSH module.
3. An integral part of the fitter's training course is the completion of the modules recommended by the Warsaw Institute of Technology

OSH at height training is for all workers performing work at a height of more than 1m from the ground, including scaffold erectors and other site workers (users) as well as those who supervise its performance. It aims to familiarise participants with protective measures and the use of appropriate fall protection methods. Initial OHS training must be provided on the employee's first day of work and takes the form of instruction, with the first general part usually lasting 2-3 lesson hours and the second on the workplace, approximately 8 lesson hours. Periodic OSH training, lasting approximately 8 lesson hours, for workers employed in manual positions should take place within 12 months of employment and be renewed every three years and for workers who perform particularly hazardous work at least every year. Periodic OHS training for engineering and technical (supervisory) employees is valid for 5 years, whilst employers, persons in charge of employees, and OHS employees must repeat training once every 5 years.

Practical OHS training during the fitter course is organised in training centres on training scaffolds. Any worker allowed to work on the scaffolding should receive the OHS training provided for in the regulations, carried out by an authorised specialist. Casual training is not legal, though, in practice, for small individual investments, this condition is often not fulfilled. A chief OHS officer may be a person with a university degree specialising in OSH or a postgraduate degree in OHS and at least 5 years of experience in OSH. OSH training can only be provided by an authorised person, with general instruction provided by:

o   An OSH officer or
o   a person who performs the tasks of that service for the employer, or
o   an employer who performs such tasks him / herself, or
o   an employee designated by the employer, who has the knowledge and skills to ensure that the instruction programme is properly carried out, and who holds a current certificate of completion of the required OSH training.
o   Standing instruction is carried out by:
o   the person designated by the employer as the person in charge of the employees, or
o   the employer her / himself, if suitably qualified and experienced and in receipt of training in the methods of providing workplace instruction.

In the latter case, the employer must have completed a 64-hour training course for employers performing OSH tasks and have no more than 10 employees, or no more than 20 employees if classified in an activity group for which no higher than risk category three has been established.

This means that any person providing OSH training must have completed a training course. As a rule, OSH training is provided by persons who meet the legal requirements for OSH specialists. However, there is no standard of competence for a scaffolding assembly trainer. The Sector Council for Competence in Construction has prepared a description of the market qualification of trainer of practical vocational training in construction, providing a framework standard from which a training standard for scaffolding assembly trainer can be prepared, and this in the process of being introduced into the Integrated Qualification System. At the same time, the Warsaw Institute of Technology – Łukasiewicz Network is accrediting examiners in the certification process of scaffolding assemblers. The Institute has substantive standards for such accreditation and, based on the Regulations on the principles of acquiring authorisations for the operation of machinery and technical equipment for earth, construction and road works, issues confirmation to external training centres that they meet the conditions for training scaffolders, including that:

•   *Lecturers of theoretical classes* have:
o   at least a secondary technical education in the field of construction, construction and operation of working machinery
o   pedagogical preparation, a minimum pedagogical course for practical vocational training instructors.

- *A degree in occupational health and safety* entitles you to teach theoretical classes in the OHS module only.
- *Practical instructors* have:
  - o at least basic vocational training, or professional training,
  - o at least a pedagogical preparation for practical vocational training instructors,
  - o certification as a machine or technical equipment operator in training area provided.

Training for construction and scaffolding supervision courses are conducted as part of the training for supervisors (among others by the Polish Chamber of Commerce of Scaffolding), being designed for:

- engineers with building qualifications who supervise scaffolding construction and commissioning daily and want to increase their competence in this area,
- OHS professionals who, in their concern for safety on construction sites, want to be more aware of the risks associated with the construction and use of scaffolding,
- experienced fitters and forepersons wishing to improve their competence and perform their work more knowledgeably,
- engineering and technical staff whose work involves supervising the construction and operation of scaffolding.

In addition to OSH regulations, the training includes elements of health and safety system management and emergency management. Improvements include promotion of advanced OSH training systems and increasing OSH training requirements on scaffolding implemented by general contractors towards subcontractors.

Current and future developments

The Institute of Mechanised Construction and Rock Mining (IMBiGS) had the authority to conduct an examination confirming the qualifications of a scaffolding assembler (keeping a register and issuing entries in the operator's book confirming the qualifications). In January 2023, following the merger with the Institute of Precision Mechanics, the Warsaw Institute of Technology – Łukasiewicz Network was established, taking over the powers of the IMBiGS including concerning the recognition of scaffolding assembly qualifications acquired in third countries. In practice, third-country nationals wishing to acquire Polish qualifications rarely apply for recognition of third-country qualifications, which can be lengthy and costly, and more often take the cost-free exam organised directly by the Warsaw Institute.

The Institute's Operators' Examination Centre intends to revise and update the recommended training programme for scaffolders, dating back to 2017, and to focus on high standards for the exam, the recruitment of highly qualified examiners and the recommendation of training centres that meet quality criteria. Consideration is also being given to the introduction of fixed-term (up to 5 years) scaffolding qualifications but there is no intention of directly interfering in the scaffolder training market.

Social partners' role in VET

Construction employers' organisations (employers' unions and chambers of commerce) and unions operating in the sector are unanimously in favour of adopting precise definitions of scaffolding incorporated into the Construction Law (and not just OSH regulations). Both stakeholder groups also favour the introduction of a confirmation procedure for scaffolding authorisations for a limited period. There are discrepancies in the interpretation of the permissibility of combining elements of the same scaffolding system manufactured by different manufacturers, with the Polish Economic Chamber of Scaffolding in favour and the Office of Technical Inspection against. The employers' organisations and the Trade Union "Budowlani" adopted a joint position calling for an update of the regulations on the list of machinery and equipment in construction, including types of scaffolding.

4.4. Comparing scaffolding VET

It can thus be seen that there is no consensus or uniformity of practice within Europe as to the preferred route, either IVET or CVET, for scaffolders, though there are some similarities, particularly between Belgium, Netherlands, Ireland, and UK. This poses a problem for attempts to create a common VET standard for scaffolding, especially if the EU is to avoid a 'lowest common denominator' approach. One perspective is to start with the 'scaffolding cycle' and to examine what it entails for the provision of a standard. The first point is that the cycle is *comprehensive*, it details all aspects of scaffolding work and the way in which it is sequenced. The German apprenticeship specification clearly does this and to an extent the English standards-based traineeship (BS1139), equivalent to National Vocational Qualification (NVQ) level 3. Ensuring that scaffolders understand and have competence in most aspects of the cycle should be a minimum requirement of scaffolding VET.

A second point concerns the degree of workforce autonomy to be expected. There are hierarchies of responsibility within the scaffolding occupation. The more pronounced are found in the Netherlands with six levels of seniority, followed by Belgium with five. Germany, on the other hand has a scaffolder and a master scaffolder qualification. It seems reasonable to say that the more comprehensive the VET for the basic scaffolder, the less necessity for a steep hierarchy, since the scaffolder will enjoy a considerable degree of autonomy due to the comprehensiveness of IVET and CVET. That said, there is of necessity a hierarchy in terms of working practices and site-based work experience because of the risks involved, so that the least experienced trainee will not be exposed to higher level and more complex scaffolding until later in the training programme, including in the German case. Modular systems like the Belgian lend themselves more readily to hierarchies. In choosing a model for a common standard, the following considerations should be kept in mind:

HOW SCAFFOLDING TRAINING IS ORGANISED IN GERMANY.

Scaffolding department, *Hansemann* Training Centre
of the Dortmund / Germany Chamber of Crafts

INTERVIEW WITH MS KRISTIN KÖHLER

Subject teacher and Erasmus+ project manager
at the *Fritz-Henßler-Berufskolleg* of the City of Dortmund

Training and further education in the field of scaffolding in Germany has only existed since 2000 and is therefore still young. Anyone wishing to complete the three-year training programme to become a scaffolder goes through the "dual system", a combination of school- and company-based training. This means that trainees, who must have previously concluded a training contract with a company, attend our vocational school for 39 weeks for the school-based part of their training during the three years of training. In addition to training in the companies, the inter-company training centres are responsible for 25 weeks of practical training over the three years.

Anyone wishing to complete training in the scaffolding *Beruf* in Germany attends the training and education centres in Magdeburg and Berlin, Weiterstadt and Groß-Gerau or in Dortmund, where we work hand in hand as a vocational school with the Dortmund Chamber of Crafts on one site and teach around 450 students in block courses. An important partner in the scaffolder training programme is the Scaffolding Social Fund in Wiesbaden (SOKA *Gerüstbau*), into which all companies are obliged to pay and which, among other things, covers training costs, such as learning materials, but also boarding accommodation, meals, travel and part of the training salary. This increases the willingness of companies to provide training places for young people and has led to a significant increase in the standard of work and occupational safety, the quality of skilled occupations, and our profession's reputation. The profession in Germany is currently being strengthened by a legal regulation that only allows authorised scaffolding companies to erect scaffolding for other occupations. Previously, there were exceptions to this rule.

We teach in an activity-orientated way in a total of 16 learning fields, which means trainees are confronted with a problem they must solve, for example, the planning of work and protective scaffolding for painting and roofing work on a particular building. To accomplish this, all necessary information must first be obtained, rules and dependencies clarified, and competences expanded. The topic of occupational safety is always considered and is anyway a core part of scaffolder training.

The three-year theoretical and practical training programme is very comprehensive and covers all aspects of scaffolding construction. Regardless of scaffolding type – working, protective, interior, suspended or supporting, and event scaffolding (e.g. grandstands) are taught here, using scaffolding material from different manufacturers. The trainees are also familiar with different wall structures, levelling equipment and the properties of different floor types. They can make static assumptions, take part in maths lessons, and are prepared for their future careers in economics, politics and German lessons. And if the qualified scaffolder wants to take on even more responsibility later, they can complete further training – also here on site – to become a team leader or master scaffolder.

The *Fritz-Henßler-Berufskolleg* has been accredited for Erasmus+ since 2019 because it is important to support trainees in broadening their horizons, but projects could not start in our scaffolding department until after the coronavirus period, in spring 2022. Despite the coronavirus over 300 student and teacher mobilities have been organised since 2019. For instance, nine young scaffolders have been to Bergen (Norway), six to Linz and Klagenfurt (Austria), three to Istanbul (Turkey), two to Paris (France) and three to Gothenburg (Sweden), all short-term mobilities, with the trainees staying in another European company for three weeks at a time to gain work experience. However, there are long-term mobilities and qualified scaffolders can also work in another European country for up to one year after completing their training, subsidised by the EU, so providing a very good opportunity, not yet utilised in our department and still not implemented enough in Europe, needing more intensive advertising.

There is an organisational effort involved, hardly manageable for our trainees without help. First, they must find suitable companies, convince the local companies, conclude contracts, agreements and insurance policies, enter all this into an EU tool and finally receive the Europass Mobility card. Even if you know how it works as a teacher, it takes a lot of imagination. Unlike at universities, we do not have our own departments or, as is the case at some Chambers of Crafts, people responsible for helping participants with the organisation. To do justice to the opportunities Erasmus+ can offer, we teachers have to be given more time off.

Without exception, the trainees are delighted when they come back and very grateful for the experience; it is a pleasure to see what a development boost they have from working in another country with other colleagues – even if only for three weeks – usually having to communicate in a foreign language and getting to know the country, people and culture. Erasmus+ is an excellent opportunity to develop the soft skills of our trainees. Together with the master crafts persons of the Dortmund Chamber of Crafts, we select reliable and hard-working trainees who, due to personal circumstances, have had little opportunity to gain such experience. Erasmus+ pays a lump sum to cover the costs of travelling, accommodation and meals, whilst the trainee's salary continues to be paid, as the stay abroad is part of the training programme, and the trainee is loaned by the home training company to the host company abroad. This means the financial side is not a problem.

There have never been any problems. The German training companies have always been willing to support the programme and proud their trainee was selected from the many   →

applicants. The main problem is finding host companies where occupational safety is guaranteed, and our trainees are treated well. You must proceed very sensitively. We teachers can make preparatory visits to familiarise ourselves with the companies. Personal contacts and a good network are helpful in finding good host companies in other European countries. The UEG, the Union of European Scaffolders, is a reliable partner here, as are the relevant scaffolding manufacturers with contacts abroad.

It would be a good development if Erasmus+ were as widely recognised by trainees as among students. This would promote European cohesion. At the end of their Erasmus+ stay, trainees complete a questionnaire in which they regularly confirm this experience has helped to strengthen their awareness as Europeans. Even after their stay abroad, many are open to working abroad later and passing on their professional and personal experiences. The feeling that this Europe is "their" Europe is significantly strengthened. What more could you wish for?

- Health and safety.
- Labour market security
- The maintenance of a healthy occupational labour market
- Productivity of both individuals and teams.

A further consideration relates to how far OSH training, which is required to work as a scaffolder across all countries studied, is integrated into scaffolding training programmes or can be separated. This varies significantly among them, with Poland having extensive separate OSH training requirements whilst in Germany it is difficult to disentangle OSH training from the curricula of its more integrated programme. In addition, there is little information on OSH training offered to scaffolder users.

To summarise the main points of comparison between the countries studied:
o *Routes to competence* in scaffolding vary significantly, ranging from full IVET qualification in Germany, through the integration of IVET and CVET in Denmark and Ireland, to CVET certification as found in Belgium and the Netherlands.
o *Training content and duration* vary significantly, ranging from three years in the dual system in Germany to short standalone courses for certification in the Netherlands.
o *OSH training*, whilst integrated into to all VET scaffolding programmes, apart from Poland, is not always easy to disentangle from the curriculum of, for instance, Germany.
o *Recent developments* show significantly different trajectories of training systems. While in Ireland scaffolding is the newest construction apprenticeship programme, in the Netherlands the IVET programme is no longer provided due to lack of enrolment.
o *The role of the social partners* varies, from important social dialogue structures determining the VET systems of some countries to much weaker examples in others.

VISIT TO CISRS SCAFFOLDING TRAINING CENTRE, LONDON, UK

Hosted by David Mosley, CISRS Managing Director and NASC Training Director,
and Kevin Williamson (Unite the Union),
December 2023

LINDA CLARKE
ProBE, University of Westminster

At the time of the visit, the Centre known as the London Academy of Sustainable Construction, had 120 trainees, including 3 women, undertaking a scaffolding apprenticeship, level 2, from 18-24 months of which three months is spent at the centre. Trainees come 5 times, 2 weeks at a time, covering 6 elements from Basic and finishing with an end-point assessment with a separate company. At the Centre, 75% is purely practical, for which they must adhere to a plan, and 25% theory, covering British values, English, Maths, costs of materials, etc. At advanced level 3 scaffolders can plan, and it then takes from 2-5 years to become an advanced ganger.

Normally the large companies provide the training, and the college can intervene in providing placements. The centre receives some funding from the Construction Industry Training Board (CITB). Scaffolding is generally well paid, and scaffolders must be qualified, with a card to prove this. Scaffolding at the centre is tube and fitting/scissors, plus some systems. Officers from the union, Unite, and from the employers' organisation, the National Access and Scaffolding Confederation (NASC) monitor the training. Scaffolding in UK was 90% direct employment, but now only about 75%; self-employment is particularly high in London.

UK Scaffolding organisations include NASC, which was founded in 1945 and currently has 280 members, covering for instance training providers, manufacturers etc. Members may employ less than 20 or consist of suppliers and contractors employing 2,000+. CISRS is the Construction Industry Scaffolders Record Scheme, involved in training in the different regions, with 30+ centres; 67,000 are registered on the card scheme. OSTS, the Overseas Scaffolding Training Scheme, is based on the UK scheme, though split into shorter modules; there are 20,000 OSTS scaffolding cardholders and 14 centres, including in Saudi Arabia, Abu Dhabi, Qatar, China, Trinidad, India, Nepal, Nigeria and Russia.

Fernando Durán-Palma, Linda Clarke, David Mosley
and Kevin Williamson outside training centre

5. TECHNOLOGICAL DEVELOPMENTS

5.1 Overview

The country reports paint a picture of a diverse and dynamic sector where not only varieties of scaffolding types and technologies coexist but also tradition continuously meets innovation in a drive for more efficient, safe and sustainable scaffolding. System scaffolding is the dominant type of scaffolding used across the countries studied. This does not mean that other systems, notably tube and fittings, are completely absent, but that their use is circumscribed to specific situations. Nor does this mean that there is a preferred subtype of System Scaffolding in use.

While the development and adoption of new technologies vary greatly not only among but also within participating countries (e.g. between large and small scaffolding companies), in all cases, the shape of the sector has changed significantly in the three decades since the First European Scaffolding Conference in 1996. 'Incrementally new' technologies have increasingly been adopted, particularly labour-relieving tools and machinery that reduce the physical strain on workers, such as electric lifts, hoists, cranes, and trolleys, as well as advanced individual and collective safety features such as fall protection systems and advanced guardrails.

The picture is harder to establish regarding 'radically new' technologies. *Drones*, for instance, are increasingly being used in scaffolding construction-related activities. However, the extent of their adoption in scaffolding varies widely across countries. While drones are not employed in Belgium, Ireland or the Netherlands and are only 'slowly gaining ground' in Denmark and Germany in terms of surveying and planning, they are confidently being adopted in Poland, where large construction companies use them to assess the condition of scaffolds, and the State Labour Inspectorate and the Office of Technical Inspection are being equipped with drones to inspect scaffolding. Scaffolding companies are aware of developments concerning *cobots* and *robots*, but, at present, their adoption remains limited. Other radically new technologies, such as exoskeletons, are under development in Denmark and Germany, but initial research shows that they are considered versatile enough for scaffolding work.

INDUSTRY 4.0 TECHNOLOGIES ARE ESTABLISHING THEMSELVES IN SCAFFOLDING

PROF. DR.-ING. CHRISTIAN SCHLETTE
SDU Centre for Large Structure Production (LSP),
University of Southern Denmark

As in the construction industry in general, there is an urgent need for innovation in scaffolding to increase reliability and productivity, while at the same time there is a shortage of skilled labour. Scaffolding construction finds particular inspiration in Industry 4.0 technologies that have been developed and used in other industrial sectors (such as automotive engineering) for around ten years in order to address the automated production of highly customised, high-quality products.

It can be observed how such Industry 4.0 technologies are first used in the production process of scaffolding manufacturers and then in the next step – often made possible by the new internal infrastructures at the scaffolding manufacturers – are also offered in the context of the actual scaffolding for use in the field – first by experts from the manufacturer and then by scaffolders and other customers.

Industry 4.0 data technologies are increasingly being used in scaffolding construction – for example in the form of digital planning tools and assembly instructions that are also accessible to non-experts to optimise scaffolding applications safely and in line with requirements. Sensor systems are also increasingly finding their way into scaffolding construction – for example in the form of optical scanner systems measuring deviations from the planned scaffolding structure or scaffolding position relative to the target object and issuing warnings if necessary.

As an extension of this trend, it can be assumed that further Industry 4.0 methods and tools will also find their way into scaffolding construction in the future. With regard to technologies that are important for production in other industrial sectors in this context, it can be assumed that aspects of robotics and artificial intelligence will be used in the field in the future – for example, drones with sensors for monitoring scaffolding safety or construction progress.

The field of Industry 4.0 is also continuing to develop, and there is already talk of Industry 5.0 in production circles, with the main advance over Industry 4.0 being that, in addition to efficiency and productivity, the focus is on the well-being of the workforce and responsible (renewable) production. Turning to these topics and the resulting technologies then holds the potential to profoundly modernise the scaffolding industry and, in particular, to counter the shortage of skilled workers by changing the working environment.

5.2 Technological developments in different countries

5.2.1 Belgium

The main types of scaffolding used in Belgium include system scaffolding, frame scaffolding, and traditional tube and fittings scaffolding. Emerging technologies range from adapted fall protection (e.g. using a Petzl Asap on a roof scaffold) and collective protective equipment (e.g., Altrad's advanced guardrail system) to radically new technologies such as Bilfinger's engineer scaffolding via 3D scanning, innovative suspended scaffold customised for a project, scaffolding apps, use of magnetic anchors. While drones are used for numerous tasks in construction, such as surveying, determining the condition of roofs, maintenance plans, and detecting heat leaks, they are not used in scaffolding. This is partly the result of legal regulations that require a pilot licence which, in turn, requires theoretical and practical training. The drone must also be registered with the relevant authorities and insured. Even if these conditions are met, it is not allowed to fly over controlled airspace or over built-up areas or crowds. In sum, legislation may prove to be a stumbling block for the use of drones in the scaffolding sector. The adoption of other radically new technologies such as the use of robots and co-bots remains very modest in Belgium today.

5.2.2 Denmark

The main types of system scaffolding used in Denmark include Layher, 8, Hünnebeck (Bosta), Haki, MJ, Stepup octo, Altrad, and Alfix. To reduce attrition in the sector, and thereby retain scaffolding workers with skills and experience, Denmark is investing in technical aids and labour relieving tools, from remote-controlled cranes used to load and unload from the lorry bed to the technical equipment used to transport the scaffolding material to the hoisting point. The lorry / telescopic loader can unload the scaffolding from the lorry bed and transport the scaffolding material to the hoisting point. Material hoists (lift or wire hoist) transport the scaffolding material vertically to the 'top man' (the scaffolder dismantling / assembling the scaffolding goes to the top) where cordless drill / drivers, impact wrenches and scaffolding spanners are used to anchor scaffolding and tighten / loosen nuts for various fastenings. The primary technical aid for vertical transport of scaffolding materials is an electrically powered material lift; material is never manually raised from one level to another by a team. The investment in electric hoists, lifts or bottom-mounted wire rope hoists quickly pays for itself, as more is produced per hour per employee. At the same time that labour costs are significantly reduced as fewer employees are needed per task, the working environment is significantly improved, which translates into reduced sickness absence and enables employees to stay in the profession longer. Retaining experienced colleagues in the profession makes investment in scaffolding worker training more attractive and provides a greater return over time due to the scaffolder's abilities to independently solve tasks within all types of scaffolding work. In terms of new technologies, drones are slowly gaining ground in terms of documentation and planning. Exoskeletons remain under development as this technology is currently not versatile enough for scaffolding work.

5.2.3 Germany

Technically, scaffolding in Germany has changed a lot. System scaffolding has been used in Germany for about 50 years and can be seen practically everywhere today. Initially, tube and fittings and system scaffolding ran side by side, but they have now been merged into one 'kit', able to erect all types of scaffolding. A role has been played by the fact that so-called 'dissolved system scaffolds' have been developed, consisting of fewer pieces, easier to assemble and having less weight by type of construction.

The rules for operational safety (TRBS) in scaffolding work are constantly updated, determining, for example, the principle that technical measures for safety are to be preferred to collective measures and these in turn to personal measures, whereby safety depends on the employees' behaviour. Technology should help employees avoid making mistakes that could endanger their safety, making it more difficult to perform actions prone to error. For example, the top scaffolding level must always be provided with side protection before working on it. Modern scaffolds are constructed so mistakes are only made with an effort and dangers arise primarily from violations of the rules.

Exoskeletons, intended to make carrying heavy objects easier, more energy-efficient, and gentler on health, are not considered ready for use in the sector; the consequences of carrying them for a long period of time are still unknown. A test carried out in Dortmund in July 2019 by a Helmut-Schmidt-University of the Federal Armed Forces research team at the suggestion of *IG Bauen-Agrar-Umwelt* and SOKA *Gerüstbau* showed that exoskeletons significantly reduced the fatigue of the test subjects; they were subsequently able to concentrate better and were more efficient and productive than subjects who had performed the same tasks without this aid. The reduction in workload particularly benefited the "person on the floor" in the chain, whereas for those on the scaffold the restriction of freedom of movement had a negative effect. That the exoskeleton could not be adapted to changing support needs during work performance was also perceived as limiting.

Drones have so far been used in scaffolding for increasing the possibilities and quality of surveying. That data can be transferred directly and without risk of error to the corresponding programmes for further processing is of particular significance for systems using building information modelling (BIM), just as for laser scanning used indoors, especially for older existing buildings where plans are often missing or unusable.

The main objectives in the design of scaffolds and tools are practicability, transportability and safety. However, the ergonomic quality of the scaffolds, especially the weight or its reduction, serves as a target variable in the technical development and manufacture of scaffolding. For example, in manufacturing scaffolding parts attempts

SCAFFOLD WORKSHOP 3: TECHNOLOGICAL DEVELOPMENTS AND STANDARDISATION

Hosted by Professor Christian Schlette, Centre for Large Structure Production,
Faculty of Engineering, South Danish University, Odense, Denmark,
6 March 2024

LINDA CLARKE
ProBE, University of Westminster

Standardisation

The workshop began with a presentation on standardisation from UEG (*Union Europäischer Gerüstbaubetriebe* – Union of European Scaffolding Companies), founded in 2008 and representing 3-4,000 scaffolding organisations across Europe. UEG also involves the producers, all working for safety, such as mobile access and working towers, temporary edge protection, and couplers. The large companies do most of the standardisation work and CEN (European Committee for Standardisation) is the scaffolding standardisation body. Standardisation is up for revision and UEG has made practical guidelines and is developing a core standard and will then revise the basic standards. The ETUC also has a standardisation unit, and in, for instance, Denmark the unions are involved. As far as European standards applied to products, Norway is regarded as one of the best. Codes of practice cannot be tuned into standards. However, with European Commission support for human-centred Industry 5.0, based on stakeholder values, rather than technology-focussed Industry 4.0 based on shareholder values, the situation may change.

In the discussion, the need for a holistic approach to machine standardisation, whether for hoists or scaffolding, was stressed. CEN represents a standardisation tool, so that a product may be approved but that does not guarantee it is fit for use. Is it useful for scaffolding? The problem is that it can be too technical for workers to know how to engage with. Such standards are not for workers but for the producers. For instance, windspeed indicators are not in the standard, a feedback method is needed. However, there are some things that workers need to know, for instance regarding machinery connected to scaffolding. There are also regional preferences regarding the width of scaffolding, e.g. in southern Germany, though standardisation allows more and more automated systems like robots.

In Denmark there have been hoists since 2000, all produced by scaffolding manufacturers, the best elevator is also produced in Denmark and the maximum height for scaffolding is set, but not in Europe. In Denmark too, weight limits are 15k per unit to avoid worker wear and tear, though it is also necessary to look at frequency. It is possible to lift safely without wear and tear, but then repetition needs to be minimised as it means wear and tear. Lighter scaffolding is better, but then there is more repetition, greater frequency of lifts.

Technological developments

Whilst different types of scaffolding can be distinguished, which system predominates in each country? What is new in DK is not in another country and technical aspects all have implications for ergonomics; workers (social) cannot be separated from technical issues. The composition of the sector is not just best practices, but economic factors are also important, the profitability of companies.

Christian Schlette explained that students work with robots and that a universal robot has been developed in Denmark, which stops if there is any collision with a human and compares with the international robot, which is adjustable to different materials. The intention is not to replace people but to make jobs easier. and for health improvement. The University works with LEGO, bringing more robots into application, though there is much surveillance involved, so this is a debate for the trade unions and agreement is needed on what is allowed and what not. On construction sites, there are many workers and a complex range of sectors: energy, transport, infrastructure, building, raw materials. In Netherlands robots are involved in building factories, prefabrication, and in France in demolition activities but there is a general lack of automation in the construction industry because of problems of investment. Drones too are happening and advanced guardrails, whilst forklifts are used everywhere. Apprentices from a company in Jutland are also testing exoskeletons, which are lightweight and good for groundwork but not higher because of the need for harnesses, etc.

The University has been working with education institutions on different activities, such as plumbing and painting, and completing a new building to support both new build and repair. It is also working with a 3D construction company, for instance in relation to installation, cladding and plastering. There must be operators for the system, whether companies, VET providers, or other education institutes. In the Centre they serve many companies who want apprentices to learn about robotics and unions are also involved. Workers are still needed and need to be skilled. The aim is for robots to take away the work that is dirty, dull, and dangerous, the 3 'Ds'. In relation to scaffolding, for instance, can robots download from lorries? Storage can also be controlled by robots, choosing the material and loading. Developments include digital tools for planning scaffolding structures including for customers; lifts, which are more and more automatic; cladding, becoming part of scaffolding, making it safer; robots, for instance in relation to the insulation of facades; scanners; mobile platforms for transporting materials.

are being made to reduce the weight, partly achieved by the introduction of scaffold uprights. In frame scaffolding, a frame weighs between 17 and 23 kilograms, whereas a single scaffold leg weighs just over seven kilograms. If carried professionally and properly, the total load can be distributed over a longer period of time. Manufacturers also report that individual parts are up to 27 % lighter than the previous generation. The perspective for technical development in scaffolding remains the reduction of accident frequency towards zero, as a joint effort by manufacturers and the scaffolding sector.

5.2.4 Ireland

The main types of system scaffolding used are Cuplock, Kwikstage, and Layher, though tube and fittings remain in use but are not as predominant. In the empirical study carried out for this project, employers stated using several new technologies including:

o *safe zone,* a fully boarded and correctly supported platform without gaps where someone could fall and a single main guardrail, where there is a risk of a fall during the erection or dismantling of a scaffold.
o *advanced guardrail,* an alternative method for erecting aluminium tower scaffolds with guardrail frame units.
o *mobile elevated work platforms,* allowing scaffolders to erect and / or dismantle the scaffolding from inside a mechanically operated work platform.
o *personal fall protection,* using a safety harness and an inertia reel.
o *safety harness and lanyard.*
o *horizontal safety lines* fixed between structural columns and used in conjunction with PFP (passive fire protection), allowing scaffolders to move more freely on an exposed edge of a building, particularly when erecting handrails to provide a collective measure to protect other workers from falls from heights.

Other responses included electric pallet trucks, impact wrenches, the use of drills to tighten bolts on couplers and fittings, vertical lifting material handling equipment, and the Kewazo Liftbot for lifting and lowering materials. Drones are used mainly in surveying and planning in the construction industry and scaffolding employers gave no indication that they used them, though some consider the use of robots and co-bots.

5.2.5 The Netherlands

The main types of scaffolding used include system, traditional tube and fittings, frame, and trestle. Several companies are using lighter materials (aluminium instead of steel) and increasingly labour-relieving tools such as forklifts, pallet trucks, cranes and mobile trailers / carts to move larger quantities of scaffolding material to, from and on the construction site. Small goods lifts are also being used to raise scaffolding material during assembly. Drones are used mainly in surveying, mapping the building including measurements and planning.

Other radically new technologies such as exoskeletons, cobots and robots are not broadly used at present. In sum, the Dutch scaffolding sector is evolving, with improvements in material used and equipment, but remains conservative regarding the adoption of new technologies.

5.2.6 Poland

Numerous types of scaffolding are in use in Poland, but the main one is system scaffolding. The so-called Warsaw scaffold is still very popular, a type of modular scaffolding consisting of a skeleton welded from steel pipes with a diameter of approximately 35 mm and lengths of 0.7m and 1.5m, which is legally allowed to be erected up to a maximum height of 8m, so only useful for simple work. The old wooden structures have been superseded by modern steel and aluminium models used by scaffolding service providers, but wooden scaffolding can still be found in small individual projects.

The introduction of new scaffolding techniques in Poland is similar to other EU countries; Polish manufacturers and large Polish construction companies are anyway mostly branches of international companies. An interesting scaffolding technique was the use of a mobile replacement bridge constructed from a scaffolding system in the renovation of the old drawbridge in Gdansk in 2023. Other developments include the increasingly popular use of freestanding mobile platforms for work at height and the use of drones. The State Labour Inspectorate is being equipped with drones to assess the state of a scaffolding installation (including compliance with OSH regulations) without the inspector having to work at height. The Office of Technical Inspection is also being equipped with drones with the intention of eliminating in some cases the need to build scaffolding to provide access to equipment during testing, or to employ climbers, as also applies to installations on building structures. The use of drones also makes it possible to carry out surveys relatively quickly and cheaply, without interfering with the structure of the installation, in places that are difficult to access and, above all, without the potential risks incurred by the surveyor when working at height. Large construction companies use drones, amongst other equipment, to assess the installation and condition of scaffolding, usually deploying the services of specialised external companies. In the case of smaller investments and small and medium-sized construction companies, however, this service is rarely used.

The use of robots in construction work is under discussion, including for scaffolding. For example, machines performing welding and painting work on prefabricated elements could be used. The possible use of robots to reduce the need for scaffolding is being analysed, for instance, for laying prefabricated elements to build walls of varying shapes or replacing a crane or scaffolding on some sites. The possibility of using drones to lay small bricks and other elements normally requiring a crane or complex scaffolding is also suggested. However, apart from demonstrations of the capabilities of new equipment, there has been no wider use of robots and drones on construction sites. Robotisation in construction is not progressing as quickly as for other sectors due to the specificity of processes, including significant variation in construction projects. Nor did interviews and desk research identify the use of cobots.

5.3 Comparing technological developments in different countries

The country reports, and discussions held in the workshops and final conference indicate that, while there is a generally positive predisposition about radically new technologies and their potential impact on safety, well-being and inclusiveness in the sector, there is also recognition of the challenges involved in their development and adoption. These range from specific issues, such as the high costs and ergonomic implications of new technologies, to more fundamental matters that should guide technological development in the sector. About the latter, participants clearly expressed the necessity for workers and their representative organisations to be meaningfully involved with manufacturers and employers not only in the adoption of new technologies but also in their conception, design and development.

STANDARDS FOR SCAFFOLDS AND SCAFFOLDING

KATRIN BEHNKE
Project Officer,
European Trade Union Confederation (ETUC)

Technical requirements for the manufacturing and design of scaffolds are often set by standards. In Europe, the European Committee for Standardisation (CEN) has a dedicated technical committee, CEN/TC 53 'Temporary work equipment', tasked with the development of technical standards in the field of scaffolding. Members of this technical committee mostly comprise scaffold manufacturers. A European standard is identical in all European countries, meaning that European standards on scaffolds need to be adopted across Europe as national standards. Furthermore, a couple of scaffold standards are also developed at international level, ISO, not necessarily reflecting European specificities. While CEN or ISO standards strive for harmonisation of technical requirements across several countries, they do not have to be applied and are therefore not mandatory. The task of producing and selling quality scaffolds that are safe to work with should not be left to standards alone. Market surveillance is key in ensuring safe scaffolds on the European market.

In the European legal acquis under the New Legislative Framework (NLF), some legislation (e.g. on construction products, PPE, etc) gives essential health and safety requirements and the technical details for these are developed in so-called harmonised standards, which are requested by the European Commission and underpin the respective legislation. The Work Equipment Directive does not fall under the NLF so current European standards for scaffolds are not harmonised standards, they do not underpin the Work Equipment Directive and their application does not give rise to an automatic presumption of conformity with this Directive. At the same time, the specifications in the Work Equipment Directive are very vague ("appropriate", "dangerous gap", etc.) and leave much room for manoeuvre. As a result, it is left to the standardisation committee and its members to define what is a good safety level, which must not necessarily reflect the views of unions and workers. Without clear requirements for health and safety specific for scaffolding, using the Directive as basis for harmonised standardisation is therefore not advisable.

Standard-setting bodies have been designed to set technical standards by companies for companies. Sometimes a participation fee needs to be paid to join a national standardisation committee. As a result, there is little or no democratic oversight built into them and unions are underrepresented or not represented at all. Non-technical requirements should therefore not be the subject of standardisation; matters such as training, working conditions or safety measures should be regulated through European or national legislation or social dialogue. The involvement of union representatives in CEN/TC 53 is advisable for those that set requirements with an impact on the health and safety of scaffolders. To reduce barriers, unions should participate in national mirror committees at no cost to them, especially considering they have no commercial interest. For several years, the ETUC has had a project that strengthens union intervention to represent social interests in the standardisation process at European level.

6. SOCIAL DIALOGUE IN SCAFFOLDING

6.1. Overview

Significant differences exist in the scaffolding sector between the countries studied regarding the strength and autonomy of relevant social partners, the strength of social dialogue structures, the prevalence and breadth of collective agreements, and the nature of paritarian organisations, reflecting in turn relations to broader national institutions, union density and collective bargaining coverage.

6.2. Social dialogue in different countries

6.2.1. Belgium

Social partner organisations

The Joint Committees (JC) are specific platforms created for different industries in the aftermath of the Second World War in which social dialogue is organised between the different social partners (employer associations and unions), with blue and white-collar workers historically attributed to different JCs, albeit working for the same company and, therefore, active in the same industry. JC 124 for construction (Federal Public Service/Employment Labour and Social Dialogue) is organised between 6 different social partners, equally representing both parties (3 employer's organisations and 3 trade unions). The employer's organisations are:

o *Embuild*, the Confederation of Construction Companies in Belgium, bringing together the different local entities as well as clusters of federations representing groups of companies of the same sub-sector including the Royal Federation of Complementary Construction Companies (Fedecom) of which FEMEB-VSBB is a member.

SCAFFOLDING YESTERDAY, TODAY AND TOMORROW: UK

ROB MIGUEL
National Health and Safety Advisor,
UNITE the Union, UK

Builders in the UK have been developing and adapting scaffolding for thousands of years. While the scaffolding we see today is surprisingly sophisticated, the first scaffolding was far less complicated. In Medieval Britain, monks were trained in the art of building and using scaffolding to build the abbeys and churches that still stand today. Wooden 'staging' was used, but these structures would often collapse under their own weight. It was not until the 20th century when the use of steel tubing (which was lighter than timber) became commonplace, that scaffolding began to really take shape and become the secure systems used today.

The scale of work required from the mid-40's following years of war, meant lots of unskilled labour was used across many highly skilled trades, largely due to lack of adequate training, and sub-standard health and safety practices were common. The accidents that occurred during these years led to significant improvements in the 1960s and 70s, which have continued till today. Scaffolding is in a much better place in the UK today with sophisticated systems and design and with much improved and robust training programmes that place significant importance on health and safety.

In the UK, the training of apprentice and trainee scaffolders complies with the Construction Industry Scaffolders Record Scheme (CISRS) and the accompanying CAP 609 General Information booklet: https://cisrs.org.uk/cisrs-cards/. The scheme covers both traditional Tube & Fittings and Systems scaffolding. The CISRS scheme was established in the 1960s by UNITE's predecessor trade unions and the National Access and Scaffolding Confederation (NASC) employers' trade association, with the Construction Industry Joint Council (CIJC) owning the intellectual property of the scheme. Scaffolding apprenticeships are aligned with the CISRS scheme and the Construction Industry Training Board (CITB) National Occupational Standards.

Whilst progress is well underway in the UK, more could be done in the way of improved design and use of lighter materials to reduce the burden of muscular skeletal disorders in scaffolders and make the industry more attractive to women.

o *Bouwunie*, a Federation of Small and Medium-sized Construction Companies in Flanders, whose members include scaffolding SMEs.
o *Fema*, the Federation of Building Material Dealers.

The three unions are:
o *General Labor Federation of Belgium* (FGTB-ABVV),
o *Confederation of Christian Trade Unions* (CSC-ACV)
o *General Confederation of Liberal Trade Unions of Belgium* (CGSLB-ACLVB).

Both FGTB-ABVV and CSC-ACV have sub-entities dedicated to the construction industry: General Union (FGTB-ABVV) and Construction Industry & Energy (CSC-ACV).

Collective agreements

There is one collective agreement in which scaffolders are specifically mentioned, JC 124. Other collective agreements apply for the overall construction industry, including the scaffolding sector, covering issues regarding social benefits, lifelong training, employment, and working conditions. As the construction industry is mostly composed of SMEs, the social partners seek to mutualise costs and efforts regarding social benefits of workers to reduce financial pressure on firms. The main topics covered by collective agreements include:
- *Working conditions:* e.g. protective equipment, end-of-career employment, travel expenses, overtime, etc.
- *Social benefits for inactive workers:* complementary unemployment allowance,
- *Hospitalisation insurance* to construction workers and family members,
- *Worker's training:* bonus to trained workers and training costs to employers,
- *Employment:* bonuses to companies hiring young, inexperienced workers long-term,
- *Promotion bonus:* financial support in case of mortgage loan,

Social dialogue

Belgium has an elaborate system of social dialogue between social partners at all levels (interprofessional, sectoral and company) and concerning different socio-economic fields (economy, social policy, OSH). This results in the conclusion of collective labour agreements on terms of employment, wages and the maintenance of social peace, negotiated through joint committees in every sector of activity. Every two years, employers and workers conclude an interprofessional agreement, whereby engagements are determined concerning the "social progression" (wages, employment, training) they seek to realise for both the working and non-working population, which applies to the whole of the private sector and offers a framework for negotiations in sectors that have concluded agreements on wage conditions and terms of employment. As social partners, employers and unions are also represented in numerous other advisory and consultation bodies, including Social Security management bodies and regional economic and social councils, advisory councils (e.g. on environment policy, education, science policy and environmental planning), and management bodies of public institutions (e.g. employment offices and professional training services). In companies with over 50 workers, social elections are organised every four years for workers to appoint their delegates.

In the scaffolding sector, the social dialogue is included in the "general" social dialogue organised by the construction industry social partners, represented in JC 124, which determines engagements concerning consultation in companies and negotiations that take place every two years on the wage conditions and terms of employment of 150,000 workers in the industry. At company level, social consultation is carried out by employer and union representatives, the latter appointed by the representative unions in all companies employing at least 30 workers. Scaffolding company workers are composed of scaffolders, blue-collar workers belonging to JC 124, and back-office employees belonging to JC 200.

Paritarian organisations

Constructiv is a paritarian organisation created by the construction industry social partners in 1948 to provide a social protection fund for construction workers. Its core tasks include the granting of additional social benefits, prevention, safety, and professional training and its core activities are divided into five fields:
1. Granting social benefits supplementary to social security schemes,
2. Granting a 2nd pillar pension,
3. Improving the integration of the workforce,
4. Vocational training, and
5. Health, Safety & Well-being.
Constructiv is financed through social security contributions.

6.2.2. Denmark

Social partners

Employers in the scaffolding sector are organised in the Scaffolding Section of the Danish Construction Industry Association *(DI Byggeri)*, an independent business organisation within Danish Industry representing approximately 6,700 contractors and manufacturing companies and a member of both FIEC (European Construction Industry Association) and EIC (European International Contractors). Scaffolding workers, numbering 2,272 in 2023, are represented in collective bargaining by 3F *Byggegruppen* and through the National Club of Scaffolders *(Stilladsarbejdernes Landsklub)*, whose chairperson is automatically represented in 3F *Byggegruppen's* congress-elected negotiating committee with representatives from all trades and industries. The scaffolding sector is defined by a high degree of unionisation (94%) and close cooperation between the social partners.

Social dialogue structures

The labour market is regulated by the so-called "Danish Model", whereby the social partners make agreements on conditions through collective agreements, covering wages and working conditions. For the service-oriented scaffolding sector, there is a specific way collective agreements are realised, safeguarding the interests of the parties through a national association for scaffolding workers, as well as local associations throughout Denmark. Similarly, employers have their own section under their employers' organisation, consisting of around 70 member companies. A joint Price List Committee with representation from the parties to the collective agreement, 3F *Byggegruppen* and *Dansk Industri Byggeri*, the National Club of Scaffolders, and the Scaffolding Employers' Section has regular meetings, deals with disputes arising between scaffolding contractors and employees in relation to the *Akkord* system when erecting scaffolding and with OSH initiatives or challenges, and is in dialogue with the Danish Working Environment Authority. A training committee has also been set up between the parties dealing with cases arising, for instance, concerning whether learning objectives have been achieved, and with training agreements in connection with the two-year scaffolding training programme, as well as being in ongoing contact with colleges about the content of training.

Collective agreements

The union 3F *Fagligt Fælles Forbund* and the employers' organisation *Dansk Industri* have one collective agreement covering and dealing with service-oriented scaffolding work, the Building and Construction Collective Agreement, which has associated price lists and training agreements regulating labour market conditions. There are also several collective agreements in other construction and industrial areas under which scaffolding can be performed, including the Bricklayer and Bricklayer Labour Agreement, the Building Agreement, the Industrial Agreement and the Insulation Agreement, though scaffolding work performed under these is erected for own work or as part of own production, thus not service-oriented scaffolding. A special area is Off-shore work, for which labour conditions are regulated by law and collective agreements and under the Building and Construction Collective Agreement.

The following elements are regulated in the collective bargaining agreement:
- Employment conditions and employment contract, dismissal
- Provisions on working hours and forms of working time
- Public holidays, collectively agreed, as well as national statutory holidays
- Hourly wages and salary negotiation, payroll, supplementary payments, etc.
- Performance pay and piecework rules
- Pension and illness
- Holidays, contractual holidays, public holidays
- Union rules, co-operation
- Training and agreements

- Trade union rules for handling industrial disputes
- Young workers and apprentices
- Occupational health and safety

Paritarian organisations

Paritarian organisations play an important role in the scaffolding sector in Denmark. The social partners jointly finance the *Industry Community for the Working Environment in Construction* focused on improving the working environment throughout the construction industry, including running the *Construction Industry Working Environment Bus,* which visits construction sites and shares best practices for an improved working environment, and holding an annual Working Environment Meeting around the country. The Danish Working Environment Association for the Construction Industry also produces industry *guides* for scaffolding, reviewed and approved by the Danish Working Environment Authority, where the social partners express their common understanding of, and provide joint guidance on, what constitutes good OSH standards and practices.

6.2.3 Germany

Social dialogue developed early in the German construction industry and collective agreements have long been an integral part, regulating the rights and obligations between employers and employees as well as the tasks of joint organisations. They are generally binding and therefore apply legally to all companies and all employees, even if not members of one of the contracting organisations. Binding agreements between company management and workers (company declarations) also provide for more occupational safety in companies.

Social partner organisations

The social partners in the scaffolding sector are on the employees' side the *Industriegewerkschaft Bauen-Agrar-Umwelt (IG BAU)* and, on the employers', the *Bundesverband Gerüstbau* (Federal Association of Scaffolding), founded in 1948, and the *Bundesinnungsverband* (Federal Guild of Scaffolding), founded in 1998 shortly after scaffolding had become a full trade or *Beruf.* Since then, the association and guild have jointly represented the overall interests of the scaffolding sector on the employer side. operating under a central administrative unit. They differ in that only companies in skilled occupations classed as *Handwerk* can be members of the *Bundesinnungsverband,* whilst the *Bundesverband Gerüstbau* represents companies belonging to *Industrie,* which can employ skilled occupations as well as being composed of industrial companies. As parties to collective agreements, these three organisations are responsible for organising working and wage conditions in the sector.

Paritarian organisations

All scaffolding companies in Germany are obliged to pay contributions to the joint institutions of the parties to the collective agreement, consisting of the Social Fund for Scaffolding (SOKA *Gerüstbau*) and the Supplementary Pension Fund for Scaffolding (ZVK). Due to the special conditions of work in construction and predominantly small-scale firms, the parties to collective agreements in the industry and in several construction-related industries developed institutional forms early in the Social Dialogue, intended to compensate for the disadvantages for enterprises and employees. Social dialogue objectives and procedures are expressed in the system of collective agreements and in the establishment of social funds, which is for scaffolding SOKA *Gerüstbau*, set up in 1981 and based on collective agreements between *Bundesverband Gerüstbau* and *IG BAU*, soon joined by *Bundesinnungsverband*. The work of the social funds is based on generally binding agreements, which means that obligations and benefits legally apply to all companies and workers in this sector, even those not members of one of the contracting organisations. On the part of employers is the obligation to pay a contribution and of employees the right to benefits paid from these contributions. Apart from the payment of wages during annual leave, the most significant regulations concern bridging payments for periods in which work cannot be performed for overriding reasons, such as weather conditions, and the (partial) financing of VET and other qualification measures.

The total levy paid by scaffolding companies to finance the various benefits paid to employees by SOKA *Gerüstbau* amounts to 26% of the gross wage bill, including a 1.2% share used for a supplementary pension for scaffolding workers, which is not processed by SOKA *Gerüstbau* but administered by a separate institution, *Zusatzversorgungskasse* (ZVK), and 1.9% paid by companies for a winter employment levy supporting employment in the winter months and based on a Federal Ministry of Labour decree. The largest part of the remaining 23.9% is used for wages during employees' annual holidays, accounting for 19.6%, which must also be paid by the increasing number of companies from other countries employing scaffolding workers based on the Posted Workers Directive. However, SOKA *Gerüstbau's* other payment obligations, such as for VET, do not apply to these companies because they do not participate in the corresponding procedures. 1.2% of SOKA's levy also covers wage compensation for the non-working holidays between Christmas and New Year.

Finally, 2.1% of the gross wage bill flows into VET, relieving the burden of training by companies, which are reimbursed about 30% of the trainees' wage (50% for up to 21 of the 36 months of training) for the time that trainees do not spend in the company but in vocational school and inter-company training. In addition, SOKA *Gerüstbau* indirectly supports training by paying travel costs to the vocational school and the three inter-company training centres, as well as costs incurred for accommodation and meals, teaching materials and examination fees. Furthermore, the SOKA contribution serves to finance the collectively agreed CVET and the inter-company training centres themselves, enabling them to keep technical equipment and the vocational-pedagogical staff in the facilities up to date. This represents an important contribution to qualifying the sector's labour potential.

SOKA *Gerüstbau* additionally has the tasks of verifying the payment of the minimum wage and safeguarding employees' working time credits, usually built up through flexible working time arrangements in companies, so that these are not lost in the event of bankruptcies. The breadth of these tasks goes beyond what has been agreed and practised in other construction sectors and provides evidence that the Social Dialogue is working to the benefit of the sector.

The central authority for promoting OSH protection in the workplace are the *Berufsgenossenschaften*, part of the statutory accident insurance system created at the end of the 19th century and organised at federal level according to economic sector; the *Berufsgenossenschaft der Bauwirtschaft (BG Bau)* is responsible for scaffolding. As statutory bodies, social accident insurance institutions are under state supervision though self-administered on a parity basis by the parties to the collective agreements, so that they can also be regarded as organisations that function according to the principle of social dialogue.

Decline in the frequency of accidents in recent years, also in relation to scaffolding, is largely due to the continuous work of the *Berufsgenossenschaft*. If accidents at work or occupational illnesses nevertheless occur, *BG Bau* offers medical care and rehabilitation, promotes reintegration into working life and, if need be, pays disability pensions. It serves around 580,000 companies with over three million insured persons and an annual budget of around €2.6 billion. The *Berufsgenossenschaften* are financed solely by the companies, whose membership in the relevant professional association is compulsory. Employees are thus insured against accidents at work and on the way to and from work as well as against occupational diseases, but do not pay any contribution themselves. The contribution is calculated as a proportion of the gross wage bill of a company and depends, among other things, on the frequency of occupational accidents and diseases in the respective company.

As well as a wealth of preventive measures, in 2019l; the *BG Bau* offered just under 2,600 training courses, with over 41,000 participants, so that every employee in the sector should – roughly estimated – have attended a training event at least once a year. Participation dropped significantly with the Corona pandemic, so that the figures are no longer comparable.

6.2.4. Ireland

Social partners

Key players are the employers, represented by the Construction Industry Federation (CIF) and, for scaffolding, the National Association of Scaffolding and Access Contractors, a specialist contracting section of the CIF, and the employees represented by the Services industrial professional and technical union (SIPTU).

Social dialogue structures

Since joining the European Economic Community in 1973, Ireland experienced significant changes in its workplace relations. Initially rooted in a tradition of voluntarism and adversarialism, influenced by historical ties with UK, Ireland gradually shifted towards a more structured social dialogue and collective bargaining. This transformation was catalysed by a series of industrial disputes in the early 1970s, leading to national-level wage negotiations involving unions, employer organisations, and government, which evolved into tripartite agreements encompassing a range of social and economic policies. However, the financial crisis of 2008 led to the termination of social partnership agreements in 2009 and, despite strides in social dialogue, statutory requirements for board-level representation in the private sector remain absent. State-owned enterprises implemented employee representation on boards in the late 1970s and expanded it in the late 1980s, but recent privatisations and closures have reduced worker participation in board-level decision-making. Involvement in European Works Councils (EWCs) initially lagged but has increased with the adoption of the Recast Directive in 2009 and approximately 20,000 Irish workers are now represented in EWCs, primarily SIPTU members.

Collective agreements

The Sectoral Employment Order (SEO) for construction covers scaffolders, setting the legally binding minimum terms and conditions on pay, overtime pay, pension and sick-pay entitlements and defining the normal working day and the normal working week. Unions and / or the Construction Industry Federation (employers' organisation) mainly initiate the process of seeking amendments to the SEO through a recommendation from the Labour Court to the Minister who then accepts or rejects it. Further Improvements on the terms and conditions of employment are dealt with directly with the employer at local level or at national level through the National Joint Industrial Council (NJIC), independently chaired by an Industrial Relations Officer from the Workplace Relations Commission and representing CIF and the construction unions through the Construction Industry Committee of the Irish Congress of Trade Unions (ICTU).

If an issue arises affecting only the scaffolding sector, the employees are represented by SIPTU and the employers by the National Association of Scaffolding and Access Contractors. There is no collective agreement specifically for the scaffolding sector nor is there any social dialogue committee. The SEOs place a legally binding floor on rates and obligations in the sectors throughout the country. However, the *Code of practice for access and working scaffolds* was the result of a joint initiative by the Health and Safety Authority, CIF, and ICTU to update and further improve the standards in scaffolding, drafted in consultation with the Construction Safety Partnership Advisory Committee.

Irish public policy tends to have a pro-private enterprise bias, with policymakers undervaluing social enterprises and the social economy compared to other EU Member

States (Munck *et al.*, 2017), despite the establishment of the Labour Employer Economic Forum (LEEF) in 2017 to facilitate tripartite dialogue between representatives from the government, employers and unions on economic and employment issues as they affect the labour market.

Paritarian organisations

The *Construction Safety Partnership Advisory Committee* (CSPAC), set up in 1999, consists of employers, unions, industry representative organisations, professional bodies, government and state agencies and seeks to promote continuous improvements in OSH performance at all levels within the Irish construction industry by reviewing performance, identifying best practice and areas in which initiatives could assist in improving performance, achieving safer sites and working together. Members include: the Association of Consulting Engineers of Ireland (ACEI), Building & Allied Trades' Union (BATU), Communications Workers' Union (CWU), CIF, Department of Enterprise, Trade and Employment (DETE), Electricity Supply Board (ESB), Engineers Ireland (EI), Health and Safety Authority (HSA), Health Service Executive (HSE), Institution of Occupational Safety and Health (IOSH), Irish Business and Employers Confederation (IBEC), Irish Water, Local Government Management Agency (LGMA) Microsoft, National Irish Safety Organisation (NISO), Royal Institute of the Architects of Ireland (RIAI), SIPTU, and SOLAS.

CWPS is the industry-wide construction Workers' Pension Scheme, providing pension and protection benefits for workers in construction and related industries.

6.2.5. Netherlands

Social partners

FNV Bouwen en Wonen and CNV Vakmensen represent employees who work for a scaffolding company or for a construction/industrial company that itself employs scaffolders. Regardless of which of the two collective labour agreements they apply, employers are members of the Association of Scaffolding, Height Working and Concrete Formwork Companies (VSB), which has a Scaffolding Companies section, including companies that focus on the assembly and dismantling of scaffolding, manufacturers, suppliers and hire companies. All members comply with the VSB Guarantee Scheme and VSB has an Education and Training Committee whose brief includes final attainment and assessment targets, qualification dossiers, and external representation, for example on the *Stichting Veilig Werken Op Hoogte* (Safe Working at Height Foundation – SVWOH) Board of Experts and Work Chamber. The business owners' organisation *Bouwend Nederland*, bringing together companies working in the construction and infrastructure industries, has since 1962 also had an advisory group,

KOMAT, with representatives of equipment departments and equipment managers, which focuses on creating good conditions for managing, supplying and using safe equipment in the workplace.

Collective agreements

Collective labour agreements exist for industries and companies, numbering approximately 800, but there is no specific collective agreement for the scaffolding sector and scaffolders may fall under several as scaffolding is used in several industries, including construction, petrochemical and other industries, such as offshore and shipbuilding. The following two industry-specific agreements apply to scaffolding companies, covering: Construction and Infrastructure, agreed by FNV and CNV with *Bouwend Nederland*, VSB, and others; Metal and Engineering, agreed by various parties, including FNV, CNV, *De Unie and Techniek Nederland, Koninklijke Metaal Unie*, and others. The construction industry social partners set minimum rates according to the wages and other collective agreements between the parties in the Collective Agreement for the Construction and Infrastructure Sector (*de CAO Bouw & Infra CBA*), whilst in the agreement for Temporary Agencies, there is also provision mandating that temporary scaffolders earn the same as those under the de *CAO Bouw & Infra*. In addition, there are many self-employed with no collective agreement.

Paritarian organisations

SVWOH, made up of scaffolding companies, clients (e.g., Shell and ENGIE), construction companies, and unions, was established in 2016 on the initiative of VSB, *Bouwend Nederland* / KOMAT advisory group and FNV and CNV to promote safe working at height and improve and safeguard the competence and expertise of employees involved, such as in scaffolding. To this end, the Foundation develops certification schemes, final attainment and assessment targets and exams according to a personal certification approach.

Good working conditions remain important for workers subject to heavy physical strain and to address this the parties to the Construction and Infrastructure collective labour agreement set up *Volandis* (formerly *Stichting Arbouw*), *a knowledge and advice centre* on sustainable employability, focused on an integrated approach to healthy and safe work and employee development. Under *Volandis*, every employee in a company under the agreement is entitled to *Periodic Occupational Health Examination (PAGO)* and to discuss his/her future every five years and, since they run a greater risk of health problems, for scaffolders every four and for those over 40 every two years. The *Volandis* advisor focuses on ensuring that employees can continue to do the same work for longer by making it less heavy and foreseeing whether employees engaged in relatively heavy work can do other, less heavy work. As noted by the unions, however, where companies consider it important for their employees to use this facility, take-up rates are higher. Based on PAGO, *Volandis* compiles the *Bedrijfstakatlas (Industry Atlas)* providing insight into employees' health and work/working conditions.

Samenwerkingsorganisatie Beroepsonderwijs Bedrijfsleven – SBB, the Foundation for cooperation on Vocational Education, Training and the Labour Market, carries out tasks on behalf of the Ministry of Education, Culture and Science relating to VET and the business community, including:
a. developing and maintaining the qualification structure for VET,
b. developing and maintaining qualification dossiers, including for Scaffolder and Chief Scaffolder,
c. accrediting and supporting apprenticeship companies, including for work placements and apprenticeships.

The Federation of the Dutch Pension Funds also funds and promotes the further development, maintenance and provision of a second pillar pension system on behalf of its members.

6.2.6. Poland

Social partners

Employers in the scaffolding sector are organised in the Polish Economic Chamber of Scaffolding, which is a member of UEG *Union Europäischer Gerüstbaubetriebe* and is active but does not have the rights of an employers' association so cannot conclude collective agreements. Some scaffolding companies (mainly major scaffolding manufacturers) are associated in the Polish Association of Construction Industry Employers, whilst a few service companies are affiliated to the Polish Craft Association. There is no separate organisation of scaffolders, who are represented by the Trade Union *Budowlani* and the Construction Section of the National Secretariat of the Building and Wood Industry, NSZZ *Solidarność*. There is no dedicated social dialogue structure for the scaffolding sector.

OSH is an area of effective cooperation between unions and employers in the construction industry and the problem of working at height is dealt with by employers' organisations through *Porozumienie dla Bezpieczeństwa w Budownictwie*, the Agreement for Safety in the Construction Industry, bringing together the largest construction companies, as well as the unions Budowlani and *Solidarność*.

Collective agreements

The number of collective agreements in the Polish construction sector is small, involving only a limited number of large construction companies, and regulations on – or even reference to – working with scaffolding are not included in those that exist. Nor is there is any supra-company collective agreement in the construction industry or any prospect for such soon.

Paritarian organisations

There is no paritarian organisation in the sector, nor is there a legal basis for creating one in the form found in other EU countries.

6.3. Comparing the social dialogue for the scaffolding sector

A very mixed picture concerning the strength of the social dialogue related to scaffolding is given by the countries investigated. Belgium exhibits an elaborate social dialogue conducted through Joint Committees and supported through the wide-ranging work of the paritarian organisation *Constructiv*, whilst the social partners in Denmark succeed in maintaining coverage of the extensive collective agreement throughout the sector. Both countries have high levels of unionisation, as high as 94 % in Denmark. Germany too, though with much lower level of unionisation, has generally binding collective agreements and extensive support for scaffolders through, for instance, the provision of bridging funds by SOKA *Gerüstbau* during inclement weather and OSH training by *BG Bau*.

In Ireland, in contrast, construction is regulated through legally binding Sectoral Employment Orders (SEOs) rather than through social dialogue and collective agreements that have universal applicability, with the Construction Safety Partnership Advisory Committee (CSPAC) promoting improvements in OSH. This is not to say that there are no collective agreements in the construction industry – the scaffolding apprenticeship rates of pay, for example, are covered by a collective agreement – but these are not universally applicable, unlike the terms covered under the SEOs. In the Netherlands there is no specific collective agreement for scaffolding but for construction and infrastructure overall, though this does not cover the large numbers of self-employed, whilst the paritarian organisation Volandis, as with CSPAC, provides a knowledge and advice centre, in its case on sustainable employability. Finally, Poland reveals a very different system, governed largely by legislation, as, though employers' associations and unions cover construction, there is no social dialogue as such.

What emerges, therefore, is a division between those countries – Belgium, Denmark and Germany – more dependent on social dialogue and the use of collective agreements, and those – Ireland, Netherlands and Poland – more dependent on state legislation.

SCAFFOLD WORKSHOP 4:
SOCIAL DIALOGUE

Hosted by EFBWW,
Brussels, 7 May 2024

LINDA CLARKE
ProBE, University of Westminster

Social dialogue at company, sectoral and European levels

At European level there are many companies where European Works Councils could be established. The Social Dialogue was introduced as an 'institution' in the Treaty, involving cooperation between recognised unions and employer organisations (in collaboration with the European Foundation in Dublin). There are 44 social dialogues at European level, three involving EFBWW covering the industries of construction (FIEC and EFBWW), woodworking (CEI-Bois and EFBWW), and furniture (EFIC, UEA and EFBWW). The Social Dialogue for Construction originated in 1982 and consisted of 2 plenary meetings per annum on a) Health and Safety (H&S), b) VET, and c) employment respectively for each of the 3 Social Dialogue industries. A few years ago, this was reduced to just one plenary meeting per annum on H&S, VET and employment per industry instead of 2. Aspects like VET and social security come under 'soft law', the Open Method of Coordination (OMC), whereby the EU is not directly responsible but member states.

The SCAFFOLD project identifies activities that can be regarded as best practices and possible outcomes for the Social Dialogue, leading to agreements. The EC must consult with the recognised social partners, for instance FIEC and EFBWW, for their opinion on whether to take over the process. With the silicone dust project, for instance, this led to a European convention on wood dust protection and cooperation at industry level through the launching of Wood4Bauhaus, an alliance of employers and institutions.

The difference between employees' and employers' interests was discussed as the traditional view of employers no longer exists - what interests are represented? Any threat to the Social Dialogue is also a threat to employers. Subsectors like scaffolding are not included in the Social Dialogue, though the real social dialogue is perhaps here. Suggestions included:
* UEG could be recognised as a social partner organisation.
* The project could recommend minimum standards for VET, such as with lorry driving, on OSH grounds.
* Skin cancer might be added to occupational diseases.
* A maximum temperature at which scaffolders should work could be set, as exists in some countries.
* Minimum requirements for qualifications, European core profiles on VET, as with upholstery and cabinet making, could be proposed.

→

Social dialogue at national level

Union density and collective bargaining coverage across Europe for construction and participation at plant and board level vary significantly across the countries involved in SCAFFOLD, as well as the paritarian organisations, including:
- In Poland, there is no collective bargaining as such.
- Germany has two minimum wages, state-based and for the construction industry.
- For Belgium, social partners agreements, reviewed every 4 years, have become generally applicable in construction.
- What is important is whether the collective agreement is binding or not, a combination of legal requirements and collective agreements.

Items discussed for consideration in the Social Dialogue include:
- Whether a certificate confirming training for scaffolding is mandatory, as in Netherlands.
- Changes in equipment, for instance, lighter scaffolding, better for women and men, so improving equality.
- The question of modifications, a part of the scaffolding cycle given too little attention in for instance VET, though associated, as in Denmark, with accidents.

Collective agreements for scaffolding in different countries

In Denmark, collective bargaining covers minimum conditions, hours, salary, etc., as well as the working environment, apprentices, funds for education. State regulations and changes are subject to social partner agreement, as also levels of VET, termination of apprenticeships etc. through the education committee. Industrial guidelines for erecting are coordinated with the labour inspectorate and authorities must comply. All systems are based on agreements. The whole system began in 1899. With the Akkord payment system workers are paid more the safer you work. It is more expensive to work unsafely, for instance to carry extra-long poles or not to install safety measures like guardrails. Pricing is the same everywhere, nearly covering the whole country. The price list is not paying more but moving the money around. They try to build more safely and the Akkord helps with this, for instance Action Plan 3 covering loads and lifting or Action Plan 4 on motivation to work. Each plan has a different focus. It is more self-governed than by law. VET also includes OSH.

In Ireland, the Registered Employment Agreement which set out the terms and conditions of employment was universally applicable till 2013 but was then found unconstitutional, leading to the introduction of legislation allowing for sectoral employment orders (SEOs) in 2015. The first SEO for construction was introduced in 2017, there are 52,971 workers covered by the SEO in the construction industry. Applications to amend the SEO are made to the labour court, and the court then makes a recommendation to the Minister and the Minister then considers whether the proposal should go into law or not. Other terms and conditions of employment at national level are dealt with through the NJIC (National Joint Industrial

Council) which is chaired by the Workplace Relations Commission. However, these collective agreements only apply to the parties to the agreement and are not universally applicable. There are new pay scales for scaffolding apprentices agreed between SIPTU and the CIF specialists sub-contracting section for scaffolding. Vet/apprenticeships are overseen by the government body SOLAS. CSCS (Construction Skills Certification Scheme) was introduced in 1995 and later made mandatory. SIPTU reviews these schemes with employers and SOLAS. In the 1990's there were many fatalities leading to the setting up of the Construction Safety Partnership (CSP) on which the trade unions have three members.

In the Netherlands, an inspectorate for scaffolding was set up with the union 25 years ago. Workers used to just 'end up' in scaffolding but now it is often a choice. In 2018 there were some major accidents involving scaffold collapses, leading to guidelines for scaffolding. There are regulations on how to erect and demolish scaffolding and what to expect from scaffolding, which led to the certification scheme on 'safety work at heights', based on a list drawn up by the sector of what should be tested and stipulating the level to be reached and approved. There are 5,000 scaffolders, not one without training, varying between 2 days and a few weeks; everyone must have a certificate, which is inspected. Most self-employed are migrants working for temporary agencies, which the union wants to be banned.

For the recommendations possibilities raised relate to, for instance: legislative activities; actions in relation to competence; involvement of workers, authorities, unions and employers, and improvements to the Social Dialogue to provide better lines for partner action and projects and to cover all issues.

"People are foreigners somewhere. Racists are assholes everywhere. Together against racism!"
Scaffolding sheeting in Germany.
Photograph by Walter Keller; third-eye-photography.de

7. POLICY RECOMMENDATIONS

Foreword

The European scaffolding sector is a very specialised area of the construction industry. Traditionally characterised by hard work, safety risks and rather unsteady employment, it has differentiated itself from this picture in recent years. In some countries, scaffolding has developed into a separate vocational education and training (VET) occupation. Scaffolding technology has also evolved, and further developments are foreseeable.

The special features of scaffolding construction led to an intensive discussion within the European Federation of Building and Woodworkers (EFBWW) at an early stage about general working and employment conditions, VET requirements and safety in scaffolding construction, as well as issues relating to the standardisation of products and processes and their technical and organisational development.

Since the 1990s, the EFBWW has repeatedly organised several scaffolding conferences and EU-funded projects where scaffolders and trade unionists working in this sector can meet and exchange their experiences. The EFBWW has also been able to derive policies and demands for the European level from these conferences and projects.

The EFBWW has now once again carried out an EU-funded project focusing on:
1. Working conditions and occupational safety and health (OSH);
2. VET and OSH training;
3. Technical developments and standardisation; and
4. Social dialogue in scaffolding.

The EFBWW and national member associations of the EFBWW, the scientific community, paritarian organisations of employers and trade unions in the scaffolding sector, and an employers' association were directly represented in the project. The European construction employers' organisation, FIEC, and the European scaffolding employers' association, UEG, actively supported the project as observers.

Based on six country reports explaining the actual situation of scaffolding work in Belgium, Denmark, Germany, Ireland, the Netherlands and Poland, an overall research report was prepared, describing in detail the situation in the scaffolding sector of the countries and Europe. Draft Policy Recommendations developed in the project are presented below for all four of the areas mentioned above. These Policy Recommendations are aimed at the various levels of action that have an influence on work in the scaffolding sector. Specifically, these are: the European level, the national level, the sectoral level at national level, and the company level. In terms of the stakeholders involved, the Policy Recommendations are aimed at the social partners, the political decision-makers at the various levels, the manufacturers of the products and thus also the standardisation organisations, as well as at the scientific community, which in our view reveals a field of research in scaffolding that has not yet been adequately addressed.

The recommendations are formulated in full respect of the national industrial relations and especially of the respective national rights of collective bargaining and of social partners in the field of VET. There is no intention to interfere in the collective bargaining systems, though we endeavour to support their creation and sound functioning. In some countries the actual content of collective agreements is far reaching, including aspects like training and workers' protection. The recommendations are not aimed at harmonising the legal framework or content of the collective agreements but seek to formulate specific proposals to advance workers' interests in particular areas equally promoted by EFBWW. It is also clear that not all proposals fit each country in Europe; some have long been enacted in some countries. However, this is a general aspect and advantage of European projects: finding good practices and making them available for all, reflecting on traditions and developments, and making proposals for needed and possible changes.

Above all, however, we hope that the Policy Recommendations will be actively taken up by the EFBWW member organisations and incorporated into the discussions taking place at the various operational levels. We are convinced that the recommendations are also of interest to other stakeholders, first for the employer side that has been actively involved in the project and for paritarian organisations in the sector, but also at the political level, prevention institutions and others.

These Policy Recommendations will be available in ten languages and can also be downloaded from the EFBWW webpage. The overall research report (English only) as well as the country reports will also be available on the webpage: efbww.eu

Symbols for the type of action and
level of the recommendation:

§ Legislation

  Authority

  Self-commitment

● European

◐ National

Working conditions and OSH

In this section: The six country reports of the project paint a colourful picture of scaffolding work in Europe. This concerns all aspects of the working conditions, forms of employment, coverage of collective agreements, diversity, health and safety, and vocational education and training (VET) – to name the most relevant headlines. In addition, the substance in terms of data and definitions is diverse and often hardly comparable. The policy recommendations of this section will deal with those aspects but focus on occupational safety and health (OSH) as one of the main fields of EFBWW action.

Definitions and statistics

There is a need to include a uniform definition of scaffolding as an occupation in EU legal acts on scaffolding. In some EU countries, there is no definition of scaffolding in applicable legal acts. Due to the use of the same scaffolding systems in the EU, this definition should be consistent with the description of scaffolding referred to in EU legislative acts. This also includes a clear definition of the term 'competent person' responsible for the acceptance of the scaffolding.

It is necessary to improve the process of collecting data on scaffolding at the EU level (information on scaffolding companies, levels and forms of employment, comparative data from EU countries, data on accidents and occupational diseases), a recommendation addressed to both EUROSTAT[13] and ECSO[14]. It is equally necessary to separate data on employment, the scale of activity of scaffolding companies, accidents and occupational diseases in the sector in national statistics.

Significant improvements needed include the identification of accidents and occupational diseases affecting scaffolders in particular (and separately for scaffold-using professions) and ensuring that reporting procedures are in place and are effective. We additionally recommend having specific records for scaffolders and associated sectors/occupations at all reporting levels.

It is recommended to have separate data in European statistics on occupational accidents and occupational diseases in the scaffolding sector, in construction and in other industries, and to prepare comparative studies in this area. This also includes where occupational accidents later turn into an occupational disease or a work-related disorder.

---

13 Statistical office of the EU
14 ESCO is the multilingual classification of European Skills, Competences, and Occupation

Collective agreements and forms of employment

It is recommended that the EFBWW and its national federations support the creation of collective bargaining structures and high standards in collective agreements taking into account the specifics of working on scaffolding, to improve overall working conditions of scaffolders.

There is a need to ensure proper and secure terms of employment for scaffolders. It is recommended to eliminate employment terms for scaffolders in forms other than permanent employment contracts. This can also be accompanied by incentives for companies providing permanent employment and high-level training opportunities.

Companies providing cross border services in the sector are often not acting in accordance with provisions on OSH; neither are the workers properly trained regarding OSH regulations in the host country. It is recommended to install a certification process for sending countries, proving that they are capable of following the health and safety provisions in the host country and that the workers are properly employed and trained accordingly.

Employment, training and certification as well as qualification requirements must be in place for all those involved in the scaffolding work process, including national requirements for the performance of the work before it is carried out.

Cross border work and services

It is necessary for the member states to introduce guidelines and establish a process and set up an authority for assessment and recognition as well as confirmation of certificates and qualification levels for scaffolders from countries other than the host country. Certificates and qualification levels must be in accordance with applicable rules and requirements in the respective EU country. Recognition and confirmation of certificates and qualification level and documentation of their authenticity must be in place before the scaffolding work begins.

It is necessary to ensure that information about the relevant EU country's regulations, including requirements for the performance of the work as well as training certificates and qualification requirements, is provided in a way and in a language that are understandable for all workers.

It is necessary for the individual member states to develop further training structures aimed at scaffolding workers from countries other than the host country so that the host country's requirements for certificates and qualifications can be met. Trade unions should support political initiatives to create a voluntary system of mutual recognition of certificates issued by member states.

Diversity and inclusion

It is recommended that incentives be created to attract more employees to the scaffolding sector, through open and formal recruitment processes, as well as a focus on greater awareness of diversity in the scaffolding sector. This will also have a positive effect in deterring possible instances of racist and sexist behaviour. In addition, it is recommended to support campaigns to attract more women to the sector.

Regardless of gender, personal protective equipment must be suitable and can be used and adapted to the individual person.

OSH and the environment

The Work Equipment Directive 2009/104/EC needs to be revised. The annexes dealing with work at a height are not up to date. The role of the different professional groups must be clearer. The use of ladders as a working platform must be restricted / prohibited during construction work and replaced with scaffolding.

Climate change will have different effects on the working conditions of outdoor workers. It can be through wind, rain, heat, UV radiation, earthquakes, or a combination of these phenomena. The combination of climatic conditions and working at height can result in a cocktail of dangers. Sound prevention measures should be set by European minimum OSH requirements and, depending on the respective industrial relations, by national legislation or collective agreements.

Taking into consideration the need to reduce carbon emissions in our economic activities, careful consideration is needed in terms of the use and reuse of materials, transport and equipment. These measures should be supported by stricter product certification policies. We recommend that scaffolding companies pay attention to how manufacturers perform in this field.

Since the scaffolding sector (transport, assembly, alteration, disassembly and use) remains a high-risk sector, specific campaigns are justified. The Bilbao Agency could focus a campaign on the combination of risks – Outdoor / Climate / Work at a height. In addition, and soon, the SLIC (Senior Labour Inspectors' Committee) could run a similarly shaped campaign.

Against the background of arduous working conditions that have and are partly still characterising work in the scaffolding sector, companies need to focus more on planning so that execution of the work, including through
the use of technical aids, is optimised.

Requirements for OSH training

The Workers Protection Directive on Work Equipment (2009/104/EC) contains some minimum requirements for scaffolders, competent persons, and users of scaffoldings. Those provisions in Annex I need to be revised and specified.

OSH training for scaffolders and users must be integral to their VET. All forms of training must take place in an understandable language.

A proper protection of workers is crucial to minimise accidents and diseases. In this respect, we need to examine whether the collective and the personal equipment and measures are of good quality and suitable.

It is desirable, based on existing good practices, to prepare European recommendations on occupational diseases in the scaffolding sector. It is furthermore recommended to include occupational diseases of scaffolders on the lists of occupational diseases in all EU countries. In particular, all forms of skin cancer should be added to the European List of Occupational Diseases. In addition, companies / responsible authorities should offer regular medical monitoring and assistance to workers on those diseases and, because of long latency period of some diseases, also after workers have stopped working in the sector.

Transportation, modifications and inspections

The transport of scaffoldings is one of the main areas of accident hazards. The safe operation of all phases must be ensured by clear advice and instructions and inclusion in VET programmes.

After each scaffolding change, inspection of the scaffolding by 'competent persons' must become a duty. In addition, inspections must be carried out as required, including consideration of the impact of weather conditions. The person responsible for approving the scaffolding must place an approval sign on the scaffolding, including information about the changes made and their date.

Before handing over the scaffolding to the user, the responsible persons representing the scaffolding assembly company must inspect the assembly. When handing over the scaffolding to the user, make sure that the previously required instructions and user information have been provided in an understandable manner.

VET and OSH training

In this section: High quality and safe scaffolding work depend on two main aspects: sound professional education and training and sound OSH training. Education in general, and therefore as well vocational education, are embedded in extremely diverse national VET systems. On the other hand, we have a degree of harmonisation in terms of material, techniques and work processes. It is therefore possible to formulate needs in terms of knowledge and skills. EFBWW shall therefore further investigate the possibility of formulating minimum requirements regarding the OSH training under the precondition that existing quality levels of VET systems are not diminished. Furthermore, EFBWW will promote and foster Erasmus+ structures for apprentices, giving them the opportunity to upgrade through having made work experiences in other countries.

VET

Due to differences in VET systems, it is unlikely that those for scaffolders will be aligned. Nevertheless, we recommend that any VET related to scaffolding work, regardless of the training path, should be standardised and certified in accordance with national regulations.

In accordance with annex 1 of the European Work Equipment Directive (2009/104/EC), EFBWW recommends developing guidance for scaffolder, competent person, and supervisor VET. This shall support national stakeholders to improve the quality of their respective VET, the qualification and competence of the workforce, and the work.

Workers and employees of scaffolding companies from countries other than the host country where the scaffolding work is carried out must have the same, or an equivalent, recognised and approved certificate, including qualification requirements, which confirms that their qualifications and skills meet the legislation, rules and requirements of the respective member states in which the service provider acts. Providing the certificate is the responsibility of the employer. This must be met before the work can be carried out.

The training of labour inspectors dealing amongst others with construction should include the subject of working on scaffolding and basic knowledge of scaffolding construction.

Based on mandatory VET structures for scaffolders at national level, it is recommended that requirements regarding the minimum duration of VET be developed and introduced at national level, both occupationally and in terms of the working environment. Practical and theoretical education and training should be an integral part of the education. The qualification should be as broad as possible, dealing with all aspects of scaffolding and the various forms of scaffolds. § 🔲 🔲 🌓

National Education Standards for Scaffolders (and related occupational safety standards) should be subject to regular reviews and revisions that take into account technological developments in the industry, particularly the use of new machinery and equipment. (Directive on work equipment at EU level). § 🔲 🌓

OSH training

OSH training for scaffolders, supervisors and scaffold users must be mandatory. Mandatory VET for scaffolders should be considered as mandatory on-the-job training with associated training off-the-job, at school, college and / or training centre and regular further training. How it is actually designed depends on the respective national framework provided by the VET-system and OSH regulations. § 🔲 🔲 🌓

For OSH training in particular specific guidance is requested, covering all relevant aspects and risks of all occupations related to scaffolding and, also including training guidance for professions using scaffoldings. VET and occupational safety programmes should take into account stress placed on the skeletal and muscular system regardless of gender and nationality. § 🔲 🔲 ● 🌓

We recommend EFBWW further evaluate whether European minimum requirements for the OSH training of all groups named above is feasible and wanted. As enshrined in the concept of the European OSH legislation, this should only be aimed at improving those systems not meeting the possible and needed requirements and never be used to derogate already existing training standards. 🔲 ● 🌓

It is desirable and possible to develop European OSH recommendations / guidance for scaffolders and scaffolding users on occupational OSH training in the member states, which include theoretical and practical elements, while improving and strengthening the working environment and safety. 🔲 🔲 ●

Scaffolding users (mainly construction workers) should have an integrated component on safe scaffolding work in their VET programmes. The training and education component should be regulated in the respective legal provision for construction workers, with at least a recommendation for a defined minimum training and rules for the certification as well as the financing of training and, where appropriate, renewable certificate rules. § 🔲 🔲 🌓

Erasmus+ for apprentices

Bearing in mind that experiencing other work environments and acquiring previously unknown techniques upgrades the level of skills and knowledge, we recommend that EFBWW fosters and supports Erasmus+ Action for apprentices on all levels.

We shall demand of the European Commission to provide more tailor-made information and support material in all EU languages for potential users of Erasmus+ programmes, including Erasmus+ for apprentices. Smaller firms in particular need easy access to the programmes and support in the application procedures. Furthermore, the European Education and Culture Executive Agency (EACEA) shall provide detailed data on the use of Erasmus+ programmes, including Erasmus+ for apprentices on a yearly basis. The Erasmus+ for apprentices must be better equipped financially and with corresponding staff at EACEA.

Since Erasmus+ can only work if Social Partners, companies and training centres work closely together, we recommend that the European Social Partners promote a more frequent use of the Erasmus+ programmes and encourage increased mobility for apprenticeships and cross-border cooperation. This mobility and cooperation should also apply to the scaffolding sector.

We recommend that EFBWW supports national social partners in Erasmus+. They can engage, for instance, by creating information points for companies and apprentices, supporting the dissemination of information material and guidance for the use of Erasmus+. The responsible national or regional authorities shall, in collaboration with the social partners, create platforms for training providers and companies engaged in the support of Erasmus+ actions. And companies shall engage in Erasmus+ programmes and offer international experiences to students and/or their employees and welcome students and/or employees from other countries in their premises, thereby improving the workers' skills and the attractiveness of the industry.

Technological developments and standardisation

In this section: Technological changes and innovation always result in changes in working conditions, whether in terms of better health conditions or new hazards, and in possible changes in the work organisation and, related to this, qualifications needed. How to design, implement and structure changes in the work organisation is therefore of high interest and the involvement of workers and their representatives is crucial. The project's task was not to recommend a lot of specific technical solutions and products but work out recommendations regarding the framework for those processes. Specific technological solutions and types of new machines, devices, tools and material can only be recommended from the point of view of usefulness in the areas of work or employee protection described. Here, consultation and direct participation is crucial. Workers and their representatives should be active participants and not just the subject of technological change. This needs specific legal rights in term of consultation on the implementation process and in standardisation as well.

New technologies

New technologies should improve the safety and working conditions of scaffolders and scaffolding users. They should improve the ergonomics and safety and the efficiency and quality of work. Since this all starts with the first step in the design of new tools, machines and materials, EFBWW recommends establishing processes of technology assessments with focus on all aspects of working conditions.

The implementation of new technologies always offers different ways of organising and dividing the work. How this implementation process is arranged also decides about the qualifications and skills of the workforce needed. We recommend to regulate the involvement of workers and their representatives formally in all implementations processes, including their involvement in the planning of related qualification measures.

We recommend that work on introducing new, lighter materials for the production of scaffolding, facilitating the work of assemblers and wider employment of women in the sector, should be carried out, including the scrutiny and examination of exoskeletons. Introducing limits on the size and weight of individual elements (e.g. platforms) included in the scaffolding system, and thus limiting the weight of elements carried by an employee, may contribute to the wider interest of women in the sector and thereby wider diversity in general.

Due to the significant workload for scaffolders related to the transport of scaffolding components to and from site, safe and less labour-intensive systems for transportation and handling should be developed (technical solutions/mechanisation).

Provisions are recommended to guarantee the co-determination and involvement of workers and worker representatives in all decision processes regarding the use of new Information and Communication Technologies, including the use of the data collected.

We recommend the use of technical and organisational protection for employees against exposure to harmful substances, such as the presence of asbestos during scaffolding work.

Due to climate change and the increasing exposure of scaffolders to UV radiation, changing weather conditions, high noise levels and the impact of harmful substances, it is necessary to determine appropriate exposure levels and advanced techniques for their measurement.

We recommend a clear limitation in the use of ladders and improved standards for the design of internal ladders.

The ergonomics of scaffolding have improved over the years but are still often not good enough to avoid related health hazards. In this respect, we recommend commissioning a specialised institute to examine scaffolding and its effect on the muscular-skeletal system with a view to identifying improvements in the quality of related standards.

The standardisation process

Efforts should be made to harmonise European and national technical standards for scaffolding manufacturers, taking into account the dynamics of technological change in scaffolding production.

Since personal and collective protection as well as organisational protection measures are very much based on diverse products, especially Personal Protective Equipment (PPE), we recommend scrutinising related standardisation processes, especially in cooperation with the ETUC. It is also recommended to establish a kind of early alert system aimed at interfering in the standardisation process to avoid the marketing of unsuitable products (PPE and products) for organisational and personal prevention measures.

We recommend that EFBWW takes stock of the activities of the European Committee for Standardisation's (CEN), Technical Committee (TC) 53 dealing with 'Temporary work equipment'. Furthermore, it is recommended to take stock of standardisation activities and involvement of the national affiliated federations. It is also recommended that national federations engage in participation in national mirror committees. EFBWW should continue and improve its collaboration with the ETUC unit dealing with standardisation and, if appropriate, initiate dedicated activities towards the CEN/TC53.

In relation to the design of products and materials, the EFBWW recommends stronger use of the Feed Back Method (CEN/TR 16710) not only for machines but also for scaffolding to ensure direct participation of scaffolding companies and workers and the collection of users' experiences.

We recommend that the standardisation of processes should explicitly eliminate the possibility of combining different scaffolding systems where it is technologically impossible and a safety risk.

Signals and warning notices are important for the safe use of scaffolding, for the environment, and for scaffolding work itself. Therefore, we recommend moving towards a standardised system for both safety signals and warning notices.

Social dialogue

In this section: Some of the recommendations regarding social dialogue have already been included in the recommendations regarding other thematic areas. In general, the description of procedures and forms of dialogue vary greatly in national reports. The problem is the diversity of dialogue structures, their advancement, and whether there is a specific dialogue for the sector or not. Therefore, the recommendations of this section are in principle general where they concern the national level. Recommendations for the Social Dialogue at European level are more specific because of its clear legal framework. The role of social partners at European level is enshrined in the treaty. The social partners are involved in law-setting procedures and have a kind of prerogative to take over negotiations in some aspects of social law. However, all is based on social dialogue at sectoral and company level. The following recommendations deal therefore with all levels, without interfering in the industrial relations as developed in the single country.

Commission continue to support and improve the functioning of the European social dialogue at cross sectoral and sectoral level. The support must include financial support for structural activities, especially regular meetings (plenary meetings and topical working groups) but also temporary working parties and specific joint action of social partners.

We expect that the European Commission is better at feeding project lines for social partner action and projects for various activities, such as projects on aspects of transition and any type of changes in working conditions and the environment of the respective sector, the preparation and implementation of European agreements, the implementation of related EU law and good practices with regard to provisions coming from EU-Regulation, as well as the implementation of EU-Directives into national law and its application at company level.

Furthermore, EFBWW expects that both sides of the European Social Dialogue are equally involved in European Advisory Committees, Expert Groups and similar structures relevant for the respective economic sector.

The European Social Dialogue shall highlight the working conditions in the sector and accompany and support possible initiatives at European level for improvement, namely the revision of the Work Equipment Directive and EU-coordinated campaigns (Bilbao Agency, SLIC) to better protect workers.

Social dialogue in the scaffolding sector should be an integral part of the European social dialogue in construction. Where appropriate, the issue of scaffolding should be included in the work programme of the European social dialogue in construction and be regularly included in the work of dialogue working groups (OSH, VET, Employment), without interfering in the competence of national social partners regarding VET and collective bargaining in general whilst also supporting national social partners.

We call on the European Commission to use the Open Method of Coordination to create and support strong and sustainable institutional structures for social dialogue at cross sectoral and sectoral level in all EU member states.

We call on the European Commission and the EU legislator to enhance the legal framework for Social Dialogue at company and workplace level and to foster the legal framework for sectoral and cross-sectoral Social Dialogue at national levels without interfering in national industrial relations systems or deteriorating established levels of collective agreement.

We see the need to generally strengthen employment and working conditions, health and safety, and VET in the scaffolding sector. It is therefore recommended to establish sound collective bargaining agreements in scaffolding sectors in the construction industry at national levels and national social dialogue bodies in the scaffolding sector, which will be part of national autonomous or tripartite dialogue structures.

Without touching the structure of industrial relations at national levels or interfering in collective bargaining, EFBWW recommends that the social dialogue in the scaffolding sector should cover all key issues for the labour market: work safety, other framework working conditions of employees employed in the scaffolding sector (primarily working time, working environment, remuneration), gender and equality issues, and conditions for acquiring and improving VET qualifications.

EFBWW recommends verifying the process of change regarding OSH and changes in technology and work organisation to identify possible points of automation, as well as verifying framework conditions such as the circular economy and climate change in the scaffolding sector at all levels of social dialogue. Related regulation should be verified, and VET programmes adopted accordingly.

Due to the increasing mobility of workers and companies, it is crucial to start a dialogue on VET methods and recognition of qualifications for workers employed in the scaffolding sector. The outcome of this dialogue should ultimately result in guidance on VET, its recognition, and the recognition of qualifications for workers employed in the scaffolding sector.

Where not appropriately carried out, EFBWW recommends including the sector's problems in the work programmes of tripartite social dialogue bodies in construction in order to take into account and identify the needs of the scaffolding sector. Actions should be taken to ensure that all scaffolding companies are covered by Collective Bargaining Agreements (CBA). CBA should be one of the criteria for assessing the contractor's tender in the public procurement system.

It is recommended to establish national social dialogue bodies in the scaffolding sector, which will be part of national autonomous or tripartite dialogue structures. To this end, national federations shall investigate the identification of social partner organisations authorized to enter into collective negotiations regarding the sector at the national level.

Due to the fact that generally the same scaffolding systems are used in Europe, advanced forms of dialogue in the field of occupational safety and VET should be supported. At the European level, it is recommended to promote joint, advanced work on European recommendations regarding the occupational safety of scaffolding installers and the development of guidance on how to improve VET regulated at national levels.

The creation and the work of paritarian institutions in the scaffolding sector at the national level should be promoted. Where existing, the paritarian institution that usually deals with occupational health and safety, VET or other aspects of the working conditions should pay more attention to the problems of the scaffolding sector.

REFERENCES

Abdel-Jaber, M.; Abdel-Jaber, M.S.; Beale, R.G. (2022) An Experimental Study into the Behaviour of Tube and Fitting Scaffold Structures under Cyclic Side and Vertical Loads. *Metals* 2022, 12, 40.

Avontus (2024) *Scaffolding Encyclopaedia: Seven Fundamental Parts of a Scaffold.* Accessed August 2024. https://www.avontus.com/scaffolding-encyclopedia/seven-fundamental-parts-of-a-scaffold/

BnF Passerelles (2014), *Les échafaudages à travers les siècles*, Album, Bibliothèque nationale de France.

Bundesagentur für Arbeit (2023) *Beruf Aktuell 2023-4.* Available at: https://planet-beruf.de/fileadmin/assets/01_Neu/05_PDF_Neu/Beruf_Aktuell_2023_2024.pdf

Brockmann, M., Clarke, L., Hanf, G., Méhaut, P., Westerhuis, A., Winch, C. (2011) *Knowledge, Skills, Competence in the European Labour Market: What's in a Vocational Qualification?* Oxford, Routledge.

Carey, D. (2023) *Employer's Position on Training & Safety.* Director of Safety & Training: CIF.

Cedefop (2021) *Vocational education and training in Europe-Ireland December 2021.* Available at: https://www.cedefop.europa.eu/en/tools/vet-in-europe/systems/ireland-u2

EFBWW – European Federation of Building and Woodworkers (1999), *The Third international conference of scaffolders 1999: results and contributions*, Brussels.

EFBWW – European Federation of Building and Woodworkers (2001), *The Fourth international conference of scaffolders 1999: results and contributions*, Report to European Commission, Brussels.

EFBWW – European Federation of Building and Woodworkers (2005), *The implementation, application and operation of Directive 2001/45 on 'working at heights'*, EFBWW Scaffolding Conference Eastbourne (UK), 27-30 January, report to European Commission.

EIB (2022) *Trends op de arbeidsmarkt* (Trends in the Construction Labour Market) 2022 – 2026, Economisch Instituut voor de Bouw (Economic Institute for Construction).

Gallagher, E., 2023. *Trade Union's Position on Scaffold Training.* Head of SIPTU College, Dublin.

HSA (2014) *Scaffold Alert.* Available at: https://www.hsa.ie/eng/safety_alerts/2014/scaffold_safety_alert/

HSA (2022) *Workplace Incident Statistics*, Health and Safety Authority. Ireland.

HSA (2010) *Construction Safety in Freezing Weather Conditions.* [Online] Available at: https://www.hsa.ie/eng/safety_alerts/2010/winter_construction_work_alert/

HSA (2018) *Code of Practice for access and working scaffolds*, Health and Safety Authority Ireland.

Milley, S. (2023) *Scaffolding Apprenticeship.* Department of Further and Higher Education, Research, Innovation and Science, Dublin.

Mottweiler H. (2020). Was ist ESCO? Funktion und aktuelle Diskussion eines neuen Transparenzinstruments. *Berufsbildung in Wissenschaft und Praxis*, 49 H.3, 28-32.

Working at Heights Directive (2009) Directive 2009/104/EC of 16 September 2009.

Munck R. Ó Broin, D. and Corrigan J. (2017) *Social Innovation in Ireland: challenges and prospects*, Glasnevin Publishing.

Safetech (2023) *Manual Handling.* [Online] Available at: https://www.safetech.ie/course/manual-handling [Accessed 27 June 2023].

VSB (2022) *Sector Analysis*, MDIEU scheme, *Vereniging van Steiger*, January.

Winch C. (2021) Learning outcomes: The long goodbye: Vocational qualifications in the 21st century. *European Educational Research Journal*, Vol. 22(1) 20–38.